Rarely have two very public men—CCM superstar Steven Curtis Chapman and his brilliant pastor/teacher Scotty Smith—revealed so much of themselves and made themselves so vulnerable in order to teach an important truth as they have done in *Speechless*. Obviously they thought the subject of God's grace important enough to do this. I am so thankful they did. *Speechless* is not to be missed.

BOB BRINER, AUTHOR, *ROARING LAMBS,*
THE MANAGEMENT METHODS OF JESUS

Speechless shows Steven Curtis Chapman to be not just one of the leading Christian musicians of our time, but an earnest follower of the Lord Jesus Christ. His honesty about his spiritual struggles will spur others on to authentic discipleship.

FRANKLIN GRAHAM

I thank God for my dear friend Steven Curtis Chapman, not only for the way he uses his enormous musical talent but for his authenticity. He has written a terrific book. I can recommend it—it may even leave you speechless.

CHUCK COLSON

The music of Steven Curtis Chapman and the writings of Scotty Smith have the promise of a powerful combination. I'm looking forward to reading this book!

MAX LUCADO

Steven Curtis Chapman is one of the few who are able to remain unchanged by fame, fortune, and the formidable forces that seem to pervade our world for good or evil. He has been and is a man of the faith. I am proud to call him a friend. *Speechless* allows all of us a peep behind the curtain of a life filled with challenge, grace, and adventure.

JON RIVERS, VICE PRESIDENT OF PROGRAMMING, KLTY RADIO
20! THE COUNTDOWN MAGAZINE

[SPEECHLESS]

LIVING IN AWE

OF GOD'S

DISRUPTIVE

GRACE

STEVEN CURTIS CHAPMAN
SCOTTY SMITH

ZondervanPublishingHouse
Grand Rapids, Michigan

A Division of HarperCollins*Publishers*

Speechless
Copyright © 1999 by Steven Curtis Chapman and Scotty Smith

Requests for information should be addressed to:

ZondervanPublishingHouse
Grand Rapids, Michigan 49530

Library of Congress Cataloging-in-Publication Data

Chapman, Steven Curtis.
    Speechless : living in awe of God's disruptive grace / Steven Curtis Chapman and Scotty Smith.
        p.   cm.
    Includes bibliographical references.
    ISBN 0-310-22584-1 (hardcover : alk. paper)
    1. Christian life. 2. Grace (Theology). 3. Chapman, Steven Curtis. 4. Smith, Scotty, 1950– . I. Smith,
Scotty, 1950– II. Title.
BV4501.2.C477 1999
248.4—dc21
                                                         99-25244
                                                           CIP

This edition printed on acid-free paper and meets the American National Standards Institute Z39.48 standard.

All Scripture quotations, unless otherwise indicated, are taken from the *Holy Bible: New International Version*®.
NIV®. Copyright © 1973, 1978, 1984 by International Bible Society. Used by permission of Zondervan Publishing
House. All rights reserved.

"Dive," "Great Expectations," "Fingerprints of God," "Be Still and Know" (Steven Curtis Chapman) © 1999 Sparrow Song/Peach Hill Songs (BMI). All rights administered by EMI Christian Music Publishing.

"The Invitation," "Speechless" (Steven Curtis Chapman/Geoff Moore) © 1999 Sparrow Song/Peach Hill Songs (BMI)/Songs On The Forefront/Geoff Moore Songs (SESAC). All rights administered by EMI Christian Music Publishing.

"Free," "The Walk" (Steven Curtis Chapman) © 1996 Sparrow Song/Peach Hill Songs (BMI). All rights administered by EMI Christian Music Publishing.

"The Change" (Steven Curtis Chapman/James Issac Elliot) © 1999 Sparrow Song/Peach Hill Songs (BMI)/Cabinetmaker Music (ASCAP). All rights on behalf of Sparrow Song and Peach Hill Songs administered by EMI Christian Music Publishing.

"Lord of the Dance" (Steven Curtis Chapman/Scotty Smith) © 1996 Sparrow Song/Peach Hill Songs (BMI). All rights administered by EMI Christian Music Publishing.

"Heaven in the Real World" (Steven Curtis Chapman) © 1994 Sparrow Song/Peach Hill Songs (BMI). All rights administered by EMI Christian Music Publishing.

"For the Sake of the Call" (Steven Curtis Chapman) © 1991 Sparrow Song/Greg Nelson Music/Careers-BMG Music Publishing (BMI). All rights on behalf of Sparrow Song and Greg Nelson Music administered by EMI Christian Music Publishing.

"When You Are a Soldier," "I Will Be Here" (Steven Curtis Chapman) © 1990 Sparrow Song/Greg Nelson Music/Careers-BMG Music Publishing (BMI). All rights on behalf of Sparrow Song and Greg Nelson Music administered by EMI Christian Music Publishing.

"Waiting for Lightning" (Steven Curtis Chapman/Tony Elenburg) © 1990 Birdwing Music (ASCAP)/Sparrow Song/Greg Nelson Music/Careers-BMG Music Publishing (BMI). All rights on behalf of Birdwing Music, Sparrow Song, and Greg Nelson Music administered by EMI Christian Music Publishing.

"Hiding Place" (Steven Curtis Chapman/Jerry Salley) © 1987 Sparrow Song/Greg Nelson Music/Careers-BMG Music Publishing (BMI)/Multisongs (SESAC). All rights on behalf of Sparrow Song and Greg Nelson Music administered by EMI Christian Music Publishing.

Interior design by Sherri L. Hoffman

Printed in the United States of America

---

99 00 01 02 03 04 05/✧ DC/ 10 9 8 7 6 5 4 3

In memory of Erin Elizabeth Mullican;

to Ray, Lori, and Alex

for living out God's Disruptive Grace

in a way that has left so many speechless

—Steven

To Rose Marie Miller—my "mom-in-the-faith"

—whose prayers, courage, faith, and love

for the gospel and the nations of the world

keep me speechless with gratitude

and longing for our final adoptions as sons

—Scotty

contents

I had many fears when I began writing this book with Scotty: fears about writing a book on a subject that I feel I have only a kindergarten-level grasp of; fears about having the time and ability it takes to even write or, in this case, co-write, a book at all; and I would be lying if I said I wasn't battling something akin to fear even now as the book approaches its publication date. Maybe "concern" would be a better word. I'm concerned that those who buy this book because of my involvement with it will feel like they got what they paid for. I'm concerned that I have told the stories correctly and that the friends and family members I have talked about will not feel misrepresented. Even now it's hard to let go of this manuscript as I look through it one last time and see all of the places where I want to tell one more story or give a few more details. Now, with all that out in the open (boy, do I feel better) please give me just a minute to tell you what I believe to be very significant about this book called *Speechless*.

First, I am excited about the opportunity this book provides to introduce you to one of my best friends in the world as well as one of the greatest teachers I have ever sat under, especially when the subject is The Awesome and Disruptive Grace of God. Of course, I'm talking about my co-author, Scotty Smith. As you will soon discover, much of the meat and potatoes of this book come from the pen and heart of Scotty. I consider it a great and humbling honor to share the pages with this man who has taught me so much, and I trust that by the end of this book you will share a great appreciation for Scotty with me.

Second, I'm excited about where this book has come from. I started this process convinced that I was the wrong guy for the job of writing about God's grace because I knew so little about it. But then slowly, with encouragement from Scotty and the gentle prodding of the Holy Spirit, I realized that the place a book about God's grace must come from is a place of desperate need. After all, time and time again Scripture reminds us that God only gives grace to the humble and the needy. His grace is most visible when our need is most obvious. Wow! In that case, maybe I'm just the guy to write this book after all. So here goes! To God be the glory!

—Steven Curtis Chapman

introduction

Mine is a very public calling, many times bringing with it a lot more attention than I know what to do with. I am, quite literally, in the spotlight. But I have always been and always will be most fulfilled as a team player. From my earliest days in Little League baseball to my present vocation as a songwriter and performer, I have been blessed to be part of great teams. I am surrounded by special people. Those who work *for* me work *with* me. We are comrades, friends, colleagues—brothers and sisters who share a common passion, the grace and glory of God.

Everyone's contribution is vital to what I sincerely want to see happen through the ministry God has given me. That is why in my live concerts, for instance, I love to share the spotlight with my band mates. Most of the time that intense beam is focused on me. Everywhere I run around on the stage it follows me. But when my lead guitarist takes one of his "lead breaks," I usually run over and stand beside him, knowing that the attention and appreciation of the whole arena is going to envelop him and not just me as we stand in the spotlight *together*. And that is just as it should be.

Francis Schaeffer once wrote an article called "No Little People and No Little Places," in which he talked about the importance of learning to recognize and accept *our* place in the economy of God's kingdom. He talked about the importance of honoring *all* of God's servants—resisting the temptation to make a big fuss over the more high-profile gifts and not despising or disregarding the less spectacular ones. After all, it is *God's* kingdom we are building, not our own.

In a real sense, this book is dedicated to that end. It's not about me. I am not the point. It's not *my* story that is important. It's about a whole circle of friends whose love, struggles, heartaches, and hope collectively put the spotlight where it belongs, on the God of all grace and the incredible way he loves his children. As people who are captured and changed by this astonishing love, we want this book to reflect, to mirror to the watching world, how good God is and how he faithfully pursues us.

I guess you could say that my lead guitarist in writing this book is my pastor, Scotty Smith. We have been friends for over ten years. As our relationship has deepened during those years, we have become more vulnerable with each other about a lot of things—our fears, temptations, joys, frustrations, and longings. It has been in the midst of this shared journey that we have learned so much about God's passionate heart and his commitment to bring us into great freedom. This book, like our friendship, is a testimony to that journey.

We originally thought of naming this project *A Hurricane Named Grace*. Scotty and I both love the beaches of the Gulf of Florida, an area that has a long history of being visited by powerful hurricanes. The mighty winds of these storms tear down old structures and in their place new homes and landscaping continue to emerge. It occurred to us, as we reflected on our stories, that God's grace is often as disruptive as any hurricane. In his commitment to free our hearts from legalism, little dreams, and self-centered living, sometimes God must first dismantle old structures in our hearts so that his new creation can emerge. The tearing down process isn't nearly as fun as seeing the new construction rise up, but both are part of what it means to grow in grace. Only as we come to know God as our loving Father can we learn to surrender with joy to the disruptions *of* grace and the renewal *by* grace. Both are expressions of the only love that will never let go of us.

It is our prayer that as you read the stories that follow you will be able to access your own, that together we might see the larger Story. Our Father is making all things new. To see his heart and to discern his hand is to be rendered speechless.

—Steven Curtis Chapman

part one

[DANCING IN THE FATHER'S HOUSE]

Be honest—how do you feel when a room full of people stares at you with big grins on their faces and sings "Happy Birthday"? Awkward, right? To be in the spotlight is flattering, but it also makes us long for the final bar of the song.

But the astonishing truth is that God continually serenades us. In the gospel, he rejoices over us with singing and loves us with an everlasting love that will never be more intense than it is right now—nor will his affection for us diminish throughout eternity. God delights in his sons and daughters.

He does this not because of what *we* have done but because of what Jesus has done for us through his life and death upon the cross. Jesus took away the punishment we earned because of our sin. Because of our Savior's work, God loves each of his children unconditionally and passionately.

The apostle John spoke of this incomparable love in these words: "How great is the love the Father has lavished on us, that we should be called children of God!" (1 John 3:1). Has that thought ever really occurred to you, even in your wildest dreams—that God's love for you is *lavish*?

What keeps us from believing that God loves us so much? Why do some of us actually prefer working for God's blessing rather than simply surrendering, empty-handed and helpless, to his Son?

We dedicate the following stories and reflections in Part One to those who wrestle with these questions. Join us in the adventure of learning about the love that surpasses knowledge, the only everlasting love. May the revelation of God's love for us in the gospel leave us speechless—that we may proclaim loudly among the nations, "Our God reigns . . . Our God loves!"

chapter one

[SPEECHLESS]

Speechless

Words fall like drops of rain
My lips are like clouds
I say so many things
Trying to figure You out
But as mercy opens my eyes
My words are stolen away
With this breathtaking view of Your grace

And I am speechless, I'm astonished and amazed
I am silenced by Your wondrous grace
You have saved me
You have raised me from the grave
And I am speechless in Your presence now
I'm astounded as I consider how
You have shown us
A love that leaves us speechless

So what kind of love could this be
That would trade heaven's throne for a cross
And to think You still celebrate
Over finding just one who was lost
And to know You rejoice over us
The God of this whole universe
It's a story that's too great for words

Oh, how great is the love
The Father has lavished upon us
That we should be called

The sons and the daughters of God
We are speechless, so amazed
(We stand in awe of Your grace)
(We stand in awe of Your mercy)
You have saved us
(We stand in awe of Your love)
From the grave
(We are speechless)

We are speechless in Your presence now
(We stand in awe of Your cross)
We're astounded as we consider how
(We stand in awe of Your power)
You have shown us
A love that leaves us speechless
(We are speechless)

I am speechless

Steven:

I was exhausted and excited as we pulled up to the legendary recording studio in London known as Abbey Road. It was here that the Beatles had recorded so many of their hits, and the week before we arrived, conductor John Williams had just finished recording the sound track for the new *Star Wars* movie. It was hard to fathom that *my* music would soon be reverberating off the same walls as the London Symphony would record the string arrangements for my *Speechless* record.

I had been looking forward to this long weekend for quite a while. I needed it to be a time of refreshment, a time of drinking in the joy of listening to world-class musicians playing their priceless instruments. I was here to watch and to listen as my friend and conductor, J. A. C. Redford, wove a beautiful musical tapestry with the arrangements he had written.

As the writing of my first book got under way, I never knew how scary a blank sheet of paper could be. "Who am I to write a book about grace? I feel like such a mess right now, so weak." My sense of inadequacy progressed as we spent fourteen- and sixteen-hour days laying down the instrumental tracks and recording the vocals for the record. "Lord, what do *I* have to give?"

In preparation for our time at Abbey Road, I sent J. A. C. the "roughs" of the songs and a little haunting melody that had been running through my head, along with a description of what I hoped Scotty and I would be able to convey through the book that was to be based on the record. After going through all those materials, J. A. C. took the simple melody I plunked out on the piano and wrote a complete piece of music I would later call "The Journey," which profoundly captured the emotion of the last year of life for my family and me.

As J. A. C. took up his baton, sixty members of the London Symphony were poised to bring to life my simple composition and his rich interpretation. As the maestro waved the musicians into action, I was enveloped in the most incredible sound I have ever heard in my life. It felt like the sky had parted and I was being drawn into the music of heaven! Words like *amazing, overwhelming,* and *astonishing* just do not do justice in describing what I experienced in that moment. I was, quite honestly, speechless.

I cannot claim to have ever heard the audible voice of God, but as I sat there in my exhausted and exhilarated state, it seemed as though the Lord whispered in my heart, "If you ever wondered what it sounds like for me to rejoice over you with singing, this is a faint hint of what it is like." How could I not weep?

Then it occurred to me: *Yes! This is it! This is the whole point. This is what grace is all about. I bring my childlike melody and my tired, broken, weary heart to God, and he makes something beautiful!* In that magnificent recording room I was hearing the music *within* the music, the music of the gospel. Then I remembered a priceless saying of Scotty's mentor, Jack Miller: "Grace runs downhill." We are the best candidates for the love of God when we feel the most unworthy and inadequate.

That day in Abbey Road is now written down in my little book of Ebeneezer experiences. It finds itself among those treasured moments when I can say with no doubt, "Surely the Lord met me there. His Spirit bore witness with my spirit that I am his much loved son." But surely God is calling each of us to hear the sounds of his rejoicing over us more often than we do. How can we?

More Than Notes and Words

When I was eight, my brother Herbie and I first sang "I Believe in Music," a song made popular by Mac Davis. With it the two of us won our first talent contest in the mighty metropolis of Paducah, Kentucky, and before long it had become the theme song of the "Chapman Brothers Duo." One line of that song still comes back to me after all these years: "Music is the universal language." As a third grader, I wasn't certain what that meant, but I liked the ring of it.

I thought of that lyric a few years ago on a visit to Honduras, because suddenly, the universal language of music made sense in a powerful way. On that sun-drenched afternoon I borrowed an old guitar and began playing. I had flown to Central America to meet three beautiful children whom my family had been sponsoring through World Vision, because I wanted these dear ones to be more to us than just an inch-square picture on the front of our refrigerator. Praying for them is far more meaningful when we have seen their faces.

As I played and sang, a crowd started to gather. Before I knew it, a large group of Hondurans was listening intently to a boy from Tennessee sing "Oh How I Love Jesus." Since I didn't speak any Spanish and they didn't understand English, let alone my southern accent, the huge communication gap was bridged by this mysterious language called "music." Our hearts became as one as I sang of our Savior's matchless love.

Music always transcends culture and touches the soul—whether in Latin America, South Africa, North America, or at the North Pole. In all of my travels, I have witnessed this again and again. How humbling it is when God chooses to use one of the songs I have written to bridge the gap not just between people but also between one person and himself. Just last night after performing a concert, I met a woman who explained through her tears how God had used one of my songs to "save her life" after the deep despair arising from the untimely death of her husband.

Each time I hear a story like that I am astonished. Never do I take such testimonies for granted because I know it has nothing to do with me. God has allowed me to see firsthand how tenaciously and tenderly he pursues the weary and brokenhearted, and somehow, through a combination of the right lyric and the right melody he accomplishes things of eternal worth.

This is why I work so hard at songwriting, to achieve that delicate balance. The marriage of words and melodies is a gift that God has entrusted to me, and I have no greater joy than watching God use the fruit of my craft for his glory.

Sometimes when I write a song, the words come first. At other times, a melody courses through my mind and the lyrics come later. When I first wrote the words for my song "The Great Adventure," I knew immediately it was not destined for my "ballad" repertoire. A quiet, restful melody just can't carry words like "saddle up your horses." The music had to make even a non-horseman like myself want to head for the corral in search of a wild stallion—music to wake the sleeping adventurer in us all.

By contrast, when I wrote "I Will Be Here," about my deep love for my wife, Mary Beth, I tried to craft a tender piece of music to complement the lyrics. It's not simply a matter of fitting the two together. When the melody and the lyrics are truly married, something much deeper happens. The sum is greater than the parts. God intends so much more than mere information and entertainment—like the mystery he creates in a marriage.

For me, music is more than a vocation or ministry. It's a means by which I come to a deeper understanding of the heart of God and the astonishing reality of his grace. The more clearly I see God's love for me in Christ, the more I am rendered speechless, silenced by the vastness of God's supply to meet my every need. Great songs help me access God's generosity.

A few years ago I purchased a new CD by Rich Mullins, one of the best singer/songwriters of our time. He had an incredible way of communicating the truths of Scripture in poetic and imaginative ways, and I continue to be inspired by his work. When I bought the CD, though, I didn't have a player handy, so I simply read the lyrics printed on the insert. Without knowing the melodies, the lyrics profoundly affected me. I remember telling Mary Beth that Rich's poetry was worth the price of the disk alone.

When I heard the melodies to these songs, however, my whole being resonated with what Rich wanted me to know and feel. The music provided a passage into places that the lyrics alone can never go. Yes, the melodies alone would have moved me, but to what end? By combining the music and the lyrics, a powerful dynamic was created that moved the songs' powerful messages from my head to my heart. The melody breathed life into the songs. Every great song has both elements.

The gospel of God's grace also has its own lyrics and music, although unique to the gospel is the way the music is contained in its lyric. *Nothing* can compare with the wonder that occurs when the truth of the gospel sings in our hearts by the work of the Holy Spirit.

My calling as a songwriter is to continue to work hard to write songs that honor God both in their form and content. My calling as a Christian is to know the lyrics of the gospel so well that its music resonates through my whole being to the delight of my Father, anytime, anywhere.

Writer Stacey Rhinehart tells a story that captures this image.

> Once when the Cleveland Symphony was performing *The Magic Flute* by Mozart, an electrical storm caused the lights to go out. Undaunted by the difficulties, the members of the orchestra knew the music so well that they completed the performance in the dark. At the end of the performance, the audience burst into thunderous applause, and a stagehand illuminated the orchestra and conductor with a flashlight so that they could take their bows.[1]

The only applause that really matters is God's, and it is thunderously heard for each of us in the gospel of his grace.

Scotty:

Good News or Good Vibrations?

With Steven, I share a deep love for music, though, since high school, the genre that remains my favorite is what we native Carolinians call "beach music." For some of you that conjures images of sun-bleached hair, surfboards, and the tight harmonies of the Beach Boys and Jan and Dean. Right era but wrong beaches—and wrong music! Beach music got its name from the beaches of North and South Carolina, and any decent collection of beach music will include such groups as the Delfonics, the Stylistics, the Intruders, the Chi-Lites, the Temptations, and the Four Tops.

As soon as I hear the opening bass riff of the Temptation's classic "My Girl," memories flood in, I look for my wife's hand, and my feet instinctively begin a dance called the "shag." I am embarrassed to say, however, that if my next meal was contingent upon reciting the lyrics to "My Girl," I would starve. I've never been good at remembering the words to songs, because the melody affects me far more than the lyrics.

The same was true of my early experience of Christianity. I had always had a hard time understanding religious words. In fact, as a child, when I tried to memorize the Lord's Prayer, I thought it said, "Our Father, which art in heaven, *hollow* is Thy Name . . ." I had no idea what *hallowed* meant, so I simply learned to mimic words that were, indeed, hollow to me. Content didn't matter.

When I became a senior in high school, however, the faith was finally presented to me in a way that did matter. I began to understand that Jesus Christ is the way and the truth and the life, and I came to believe that the gospel is the *good news* of the revelation of Jesus Christ. I began a lifelong surrender of my mind and emotions in the late sixties to him who alone is worthy. My head and heart found a resting place in the truth and grace of Jesus. But little did I realize then how much I still had to learn.

Mean Christians in an Age of Spiritual Hunger

Still, as a young Christian, it did not take me long to encounter a large and vocal group of Christians who had tons of biblical knowledge but were spiritually flat—even mean at times. Though I had all the arrogance of a new convert, still I struggled to understand how these believers could have so little awe of the wonderful truths they were so zealous to defend and protect. *Where is their joy? Their love?* I often wondered.

For instance, soon after I became a Christian, my friend Wade, an amazing rock-and-roll guitarist in a local band, began to wonder whether this "Jesus thing" offered him anything of substance. One night, as his hunger to know God intensified, he decided to attend a little church that had a sign out front, announcing, "Revival in Progress!" He sheepishly took a seat in the back of the chapel, feeling out of place in his faded blue jeans and shoulder-length blond hair.

The sermon, according to Wade, was little more than a tirade against liberals, communists, hippies, and people who used any translation of the Bible other than the King James. Nevertheless, Wade responded to the altar call at the end of the service. Walking to the front of the packed auditorium, with a sincere desire to have the evangelist pray with him, my friend received this greeting: "Son, what're you doing here? Go cut your hair, come back, and *then* we can talk about Jesus." When Wade told me this story, I was furious. Fortunately, his hunger for grace outweighed the wounding his heart took that night. He became a Christian within a couple of weeks.

This represented my first putrid taste of intellectual Pharisaism, the dangerous illusion of confusing knowledge with spirituality. I remember thinking, "If that's what theology does to Christians, then don't give me theology, just give me Jesus." Believers who talked, lived, and prayed with fire and joy commanded my respect a lot more than those biblical hairsplitters. If forced to choose between dead orthodoxy and live heterodoxy, I was determined to choose live heterodoxy every time. I didn't realize then, however, that I had other options.

In the years that followed, my spiritual journey swung between those extremes. As a religion major at the University of North Carolina, I discovered the importance of an intellectual defense of the faith. I read books on apologetics and listened to tapes by speakers who assured me being a Christian does not mean you commit cerebral suicide.

About that time, though, I also had my first encounter with the charismatic renewal movement, an encounter that introduced me to a depth of experiential worship and communion with God that satisfied something deep within my soul.

Don't Think—Just Feel

"Trust me. You're going to love this group of Christians," my friend pleaded as she tried to persuade me to attend my first charismatic gathering with her. I had never dated a Christian before, so I decided the risk would be worth the prospect of more dates. We entered a large ballroom after the meeting had begun. Soft, lilting music filled the banquet hall as hundreds of Christians stood on their feet, most with eyes closed and hands raised, swaying to the soothing sounds of repetitive praise choruses.

These believers both captivated and confused me. But the beauty of seeing so many Christians, young and old, wealthy and poor, black and white, in such unison and peace before the Lord transcended the weirdness. I didn't understand what I observed, but I couldn't deny its attraction.

After the speaker finished, he invited all those longing to be filled with the Spirit to come forward. He stressed the importance of getting over our theological and biblical hang-ups. "Most of you have been under men who had studied at cemeteries called seminaries. They are dead men with dry bones. This is a movement of the Spirit. Just open yourselves up. Stop thinking and start believing."

When he said that, a little alarm went off inside me. I wanted these believers' passion and love for God, but did it only come at the expense of not thinking? I left that night convinced of the reality of their experience but also sad at the cynical disdain for Christians with thinking minds. Nevertheless, I continued to hang out with charismatic believers.

Unfortunately, this meant that I now had two sets of Christian friends. The first, my Francis Schaeffer and C. S. Lewis buddies, loved to think great thoughts and engage in apologetics with the nonbelieving culture. Then there were my charismatic brothers and sisters who were passionate about feeling the presence and seeing the power of God through the work of the Spirit. It was both painful and confusing to have those I loved and respected in each group warn me against the other. "Scotty, watch out for those charismatics. Next thing you know, they'll have you speaking in tongues and casting out demons." "Scotty, give up the idolatry of your mind. Yield to the Spirit.

You're missing the beginning of the Third Wave of the Holy Spirit, and you may not be able to stand in the last days without his power."

Only after living for a long time as a spiritual schizophrenic did I discover that the lyrics and the music of the Gospel of Jesus Christ, to use Steven's image, are meant to be joined together in one great song.

Over the years I began to identify several false dichotomies that fed my spiritual schizophrenia. As I matured in the faith, I started to see these things, not as discordant notes, but as harmonies. Consider some of these dichotomies that are really unities:

Revering Jesus and Loving Jesus
Being a Student and Being a Worshiper
Defending the Faith and Delighting in the Faith
Identifying False Teachings and Enjoying Good Teaching
Head Engaged and Hands Uplifted
Serving the Lord and Enjoying the Lord
Knowing Theology and Knowing God
Testing the Spirits and Being Filled with the Spirit
Knowing God as Sovereign Lord and Knowing God as Abba, Father
Gospel Precision and Gospel Astonishment

When I allowed these seeming dichotomies to exist as complementary realities, the lyrics and the music of the gospel suddenly came together in my life.

The Lyrics and Music of the Gospel in Balance and Harmony

Though the route has been different, both Steven and I have found the apostle Paul to be the clearest teacher of how both parts of the gospel's song are to be manifest in a believer's heart, church, family, and vocation. What is impressive about Paul is the way the music of the gospel captured his heart. He is overwhelmed at the goodness of the Good News. In Paul's writings we learn that the gospel is not merely cerebral, but also celebrative!

Toward the *end* of his earthly life, after walking with Jesus for over thirty years, Paul could say,

> I thank Christ Jesus our Lord, who has given me strength, that he considered me faithful, appointing me to his service. Even though I was once a blasphemer and a persecutor and a violent man, I was shown mercy because I acted in ignorance and unbelief. The grace of our Lord was poured out on me abundantly, along with the faith and love that are in Christ Jesus. Here is a trustworthy saying that deserves full acceptance: Christ Jesus came into the world to save sinners—of whom I am the worst. (1 Tim. 1:12–15)

Can you hear the song in Paul's heart—the gratitude, the peace, the joy? This is a man whose whole being has been set free by the truth of what he believes. He knew himself to be so unworthy, so ill-deserving of God's love and yet so fully beloved in Christ. On the road to Damascus, as he prepared to arrest more Christians and destroy the church of Jesus, the love of God literally captured him, and he was saved by a torrential outpouring of God's grace. God is not miserly with his mercy and love.

As he grew older, Paul continued to affirm the one true lyric and the glorious music of this gospel. Paul loved the meat of the gospel and savored its sweet taste and glorious aroma. We are called to do the same—it's just like eating great crab cakes at Picolos Restaurant!

Steven's family and mine were enjoying the beautiful beaches of the Florida Gulf one summer. We decided to meet for a night out at our favorite restaurant in Grayton Beach called Picolos. Grayton Beach is known for two things: first, it is the lightning-strike capital of the United States. Second, its little Bohemian restaurant serves the most incredible crab cakes in the universe, not just in the whole state of Florida.

Friends warned us to get there early because they often quickly sell out of the house specialty, which is served only on Fridays and Saturdays. We placed our order, and before long our waitress returned with four huge plates of salad, garlic mashed potatoes, and two big, succulent crab cakes, whose smell alone was worth the price of the meal. When we put that first bite of crab cake into our mouths, you would have thought we had just seen a beatific vision. It was culinary music! We moaned and sighed in four-part harmony. We closed our eyes and sank into our seats. "Can you believe this? Have you ever tasted anything as sweet, as good, as incredible? Now *this* is the mother of all crab cakes!" I'm not sure what those close to our table must have thought of our carrying on. None of us really cared. We were set free!

As with Picolos' crab cakes, so too with the gospel—deep satisfaction comes to those who partake, music to those who feast, dancing to those who linger at the table. In one of the great gospel invitations in the Old Testament, God's grace is presented as a life-giving buffet of his love and provision. A massive banquet of delight is offered to the hungry and thirsty. The price of the meal is our thirst, hunger, and poverty.

> Come, all you who are thirsty, come to the waters; and you who have no money, come, buy and eat! Come, buy wine and milk without money and without cost. Why spend money on what is not bread, and your labor on what does not satisfy? Listen, listen to me, and eat what is good, and your soul will delight in the richest of fare. Give ear and come to me; hear me, that your soul may live. (Isa. 55:1–3)

Come and dine!

The Invitation

In the palace in the land of mercy
The King looked out from His throne
He saw the sick and the homeless and hungry
He saw me lost and without hope
And moved with compassion
He sent out His only Son
With the invitation to come

This is your invitation

Come just the way you are
Come find what your soul has been longing for
Come find your peace
Come join the feast
Come in, this is your invitation

So I stood outside the gates and trembled
In my rags of unworthiness
Afraid to even stand at a distance
In the presence of holiness
But just as I turned to go
The gates swung open wide
And the King and His only Son
They invited me inside

So now will you come with me
To where the gates swing open wide
The King and His only Son
Are inviting us inside

This is our invitation
Come sinner as you are
Come find what your soul has been longing for
Come find your peace
Come join the feast
Come in, this is your invitation
This is our invitation
This is the invitation

chapter two

[THE DANCE OF THE LORD]

Lord of the Dance

On the banks of the Tennessee River in a small Kentucky
town
I drew my first breath one cold November morning
And before my feet had even touched the ground
With the doctors and the nurses gathered around
I started the dance
A little boy full of wide-eyed wonder foot loose and
fancy free
But it would happen as it does for every dancer
That I'd stumble on a truth I could not see
And find a longing deep inside of me saying
I am the heart, I need the heartbeat I am the eyes,
I need the sight
I realize that I am just the body I need the life
I move my feet I go through the motions
But who'll give purpose to chance
I am the dancer I need the Lord of the dance
The world beneath us spins in circles
And this life makes us twist and turn and sway
But we were made for more than rhythm with no reason
By the one who moves with passion and with Grace
As He dances over all that He has made
I am the heart He is the heartbeat
I am the eyes He is the sight
I see clearly I am just the body He is the life
I move my feet I go through the motions
But He gives purpose to chance I am the dancer
He is the Lord of the dance

Steven:

My song "Lord of the Dance" might suggest I have an affinity for dancing. While I was required to clog (a type of Appalachian folk dance, using elements of tap and square dance) while performing at an amusement park in Nashville, I can assure you that I have no dancing abilities. Just ask the poor woman who had the arduous task of teaching both my left feet to clog.

I first discovered my deficiency when I was thirteen and attended my first school dance. My mom drove me to Holly Delaney's door where I nervously gave her a corsage and told her how nice she looked. Then, after a silent drive that seemed to last for hours, we were dropped off at the Snowball Dance for what promised to be an evening of terror. As soon as we walked into the room, I found a seat that was a safe distance from the dance floor and glued my backside to the chair. The smooth John Travolta dance moves that my brother Herbie had taught me earlier might have looked good in front of the mirror, but the longer I watched, the clearer it became that neither I nor my Herbie Travolta moves belonged anywhere near that floor.

I sat for two miserable hours, feeling left out but determined not to humiliate myself by looking as silly as my friends did. I had just about made it through the whole night without leaving my seat, except to visit the punch bowl, when one of my buddies began to use every tactic in the thirteen-year-old handbook, from calling me chicken to the dreaded double-dog-dare, and somehow coerced me out onto the floor. It was then that I discovered that the only thing worse than sitting on my seat watching a dance was standing still in the middle of a dance floor, so I reluctantly started to shuffle my lead feet.

Suddenly I began to notice a strange sound I hadn't heard up to that point—the sound of music playing! I had been so concerned about looking silly that I hadn't noticed the music. C. S. Lewis once said, "As long as you notice, and have to count the steps, you are not yet dancing, but only learning to dance."[1]

Not until I had taken that terrible first step had I heard it, and then a strange thing started to happen. Slowly, I began to move in rhythm with the music, and before I knew it, I was jumping to the beat with my friends, looking just as goofy as I had feared I would, but it didn't seem to matter because now I could hear the music and now I had a reason to dance.

Remembering that experience makes me wonder: Why are some Christians alive to the music of the gospel, reverberating in the chambers of their hearts, while others seem to be tone-deaf to its liberating melodies? How is it possible to sing "Amazing Grace" with so little amazement, or "Jesus I Am Resting, Resting" with a restless heart? What determines whether a believer dances to the music at the Father's party or despises the sound of the band?

Amazing Grace

When I was seven years old, I first heard the music that invited me to the dance of God's grace. Although I didn't know what to call it at the time, it was the sweet sound of grace that drew me to the realization of my need for a Savior. My parents had both grown up attending church and had made professions of faith as children. By the time I arrived, however, our family's spiritual involvement consisted of my mother dressing brother Herb and me up in our church clothes and taking us to Sunday school at Olivet Baptist Church while Dad slept in.

Then a miracle happened. Our church announced a "Laymen's Revival," which meant that the visiting revivalists would need a place to stay. Revival leaders were not full-time evangelists or preachers, but rather men and women from all different walks of life who would travel from town to town to share their personal testimonies of faith in Christ.

At my mother's request, Dad allowed one of the men on the revival team to stay in our house. As a result, the gentle spirit of a dentist from Louisville, named Findley Baird, caused the sound of grace to come alive in our home, and by the end of that week my parents and my brother had responded to the gospel. I began to notice

31

changes around our house. We began to pray together as a family and attend church together, and I began to hear talk about what it meant to have a personal relationship with Jesus Christ.

Then, one Sunday morning when I was eight, I listened to our pastor, Rev. McMichael, talk about Jesus standing at the door of our hearts and knocking (Rev. 3:20). In my heart it felt more like a pounding than a knocking, and I prayed to Jesus Christ to "please forgive me of my sins and to come into my heart." That day, something in me changed. I began to hear the distant tones of music.

Still, my newborn ears couldn't fully appreciate the music blaring in heaven. The lost sheep had been found and a party was being thrown there, the likes of which we have never experienced on earth, as God himself danced and rejoiced over me. Tears fill my eyes even now as I feel the weight of these words I write. My heart wells up with gratitude that God would be so gracious toward me. What I didn't know when I responded to the Good News of God's love was just how bad the bad news is. At eight, I couldn't fathom the depths of the sin God had pardoned in my soul. I have only begun to be awestruck with the beauty of the music of the gospel and moved to the point of dancing as I come to know how deathly silent the soul is apart from the grace of God.

Scotty:

Another Reluctant Dancer

"Sweetheart, how would you like to do something exciting this summer?" Why did I feel like a setup was coming? "Next Tuesday, I want to take you to a *dancing class*—"

She could hardly get the words out before I responded the way any normal eleven-year-old would: "Dancing class—Mom—do I *have* to?"

When she said I'd be taking ballroom dancing lessons, I thought she meant "barroom" dancing. Conflicting images of a ballet bar along a mirrored wall and honky-tonk piano music from cowboy movies came to mind. Would I wear a tutu or spurs? I don't recall what bribe my mother offered me to go, but it obviously worked.

The first night of class I realized that ballroom dancing was precisely the stuff I had laughed at on the *Lawrence Welk Show.* "Mom's going to have to quadruple her bribe if she thinks I'm staying here." Of course, there were two girls for every guy in my class, but with a sigh, I resigned myself to my fate and got started.

Not being naturally coordinated, it took a while to get my brain and feet in sync with the music. The fox trot didn't do a thing for me. Waltzing made me feel as though I were stuck in a *Gone With the Wind* time warp. The cha-cha kept running through my head at night—its monotonous tempo robbing me of sleep.

But one night—one blessed night—our dance instructor announced, "This evening we're going to learn a dance your brothers and sisters do: the shag." She put on a 45 rpm record of a song entitled "Miss Grace" by a group called the Tymes. As soon as I heard the opening bars, I entered a whole new zone! The music seized me and I became Fred Astaire with Weejuns on! Finally, I had found a rhythm that matched something deep in my soul.

No more paralyzing self-consciousness or awkwardness on the dance floor for me! I grabbed my partner's hand and learned all kinds of steps, crossovers, and spins! From that night on beach music and the beach step became so much more than a mere form of entertainment. I discovered a new language and passion. These songs with lyrics about basic uncomplicated joys of life, with easy melodies and an alluring "shuffle beat," became a means to express the deep longings of my heart.

It's Fun to Dance at the YMCA

Throughout my high school years our local YMCA sponsored beach music dances every Saturday night. We danced to the music of such live bands as the Inmen Ltd. (my brother's band), Willie T and the Magnificents, the Embers, and the Fabulous Five. I lived for these dances.

During my senior year, I actually became the organist for one of these bands, the Originals (not a very original name!). We played for fraternity parties up and down the East Coast and at clubs in the Carolinas. I lived out the fantasy of so many of my adolescent peers—money, nonstop partying, popularity, and little responsibility. What a life! I continued to dance to my favorite music and make the music that caused others to dance.

Why, then, did I gradually begin to feel dead inside? Beach music, like any other drug, started to lose its magical power. "Maybe I'm just bored," I figured. "We just need to learn some new tunes and play for some different crowds." How disillusioning it is to get what you crave for only to have your hunger and thirst intensified. Soon it started taking more energy to keep up the charade of happiness while having less and less power to deny the not-so-hidden emptiness of my heart. So I added a new spin to my dancing.

Opening the medicine cabinet like a mischievous little boy, I took a bottle of cough syrup from home on the night we played for a dance at the Y. What was I thinking? Screwing off the cap I guzzled it down, chasing the horrid-tasting stuff with cheap beer. But the high carried me through our last set of songs.

After the dance I became deathly sick. My abdomen convulsed, and the dry heaves momentarily humbled me. I vowed that I would never get this sick again. By the next morning, I had forgotten my night of misery. Another day, another dance. I continued to use alcohol and rock music to disguise my insecurities and numb the pain in my soul. The void in my heart that beach music had temporarily filled demanded something else and something more. Fortunately, I would soon encounter a different kind of music and learn a dance step like no other.

A Trophy Case of Grace

One Monday morning, as I walked through the lobby of our school, still high from playing two fraternity parties over the weekend, my spirits were buoyed. Like a hunter returning with game, I looked forward to impressing my friends each Monday with my exploits. I loved to talk about the girls, the booze, the wildness of the party, and how we "blew some other band away." But like the fisherman who exaggerates the size of the one that got away, most of my stories were embellished.

As I stood in front of our trophy case, on the lookout for my envious buddies, a close friend named Steve approached me with a determined look in his eye. "Scotty, I met a new friend over the weekend."

"Great," I answered. "What's she look like? She a good kisser?" We were in the habit of dating each other's girlfriends so it seemed like a reasonable question.

"No, it's not like that," and Steve told me about going to a Fellowship of Christian Athletes weekend where he had been introduced to a "personal relationship with Christ."

I felt embarrassed and angry as he talked. Embarrassed because we were standing in the coolest place at school—not a place to talk about God (not that we talked about God any other place). Angry because he insinuated that he now had something I didn't. *Who does he think he is?* I thought. *I believe in God. I'm just not fanatic about it.*

For two weeks I avoided Steve, but he continued to pursue me. "There's a movie I'd like to take you and a couple other guys to this Friday. Scotty, can I pick you up?" Of all times for our band to have a free weekend! So, with no excuse, I went.

As I sat in the theater, the grade-B black-and-white film began to roll. I already felt weird, wondering what Steve had in mind in bringing my friends to this artless flick, but when the actors began to deliver the cheesiest script I ever heard, I wanted to walk out. College-age men with crew cuts strummed flattop guitars on the beach and sang about God, while girls wearing poodle skirts and pedal pushers listened raptly—give me a break! I thought to myself, *It's 1968, I'm cool, and I play in a band. What's with this?* But the longer I watched the more I got drawn into the story. Something began to click. Something riveted me to my seat.

Toward the end, Billy Graham appeared on the screen and gave a simple gospel presentation. "We have a big sin problem, and God sent his Son, Jesus, to take care of that problem. His death upon the cross has accomplished for you what you could never do for yourself. Acknowledge your sin, believe in God's Son, and be saved by his grace. He loves you."

The "something" that had been stirring in my guts got more intense. As Dr. Graham continued, in his own simple and gracious way, the Holy Spirit brought his words home like a hammer to my heart. "The Bible says, 'All have sinned and fall short of the glory of God. The wages of sin is death but the free gift of God is eternal life through Jesus Christ our Lord.' Is he your Lord? Is he *your* Savior? Have you received this free gift?" My heart started beating faster and faster. *Why do I feel like Billy Graham is talking directly to me? What's going on inside me?* I felt horrible and encouraged at the same time. The last twelve months of band life passed in front of my eyes—the drinking, partying, all the stupid and dangerous choices I had made. My heart beat even faster. A profound sense of urgency strangely mixed with hope took over.

After the movie, a local pastor stood up and invited anyone desiring prayer to come to the front of the theater after he said a closing prayer. I shot up out of my chair before he could say "Amen." It took a nanosecond to get to the front of that old theater.

"What can I do for you, son?" the counselor asked.

"I'm not really sure," I responded. "I believe in God. I have all of my life. I have never thought of myself as anything other than a Christian. I believe that Jesus is the Savior of the world and the Son of God and all of that stuff, but this is so different. I want to know God personally like my friend does. I want this 'gift' Dr. Graham talked about. I really want to believe God loves and accepts me just as I am. I have made a colossal mess of my life. Can you help me?"

As we talked, for the *first* time in my life I knew myself to be a sinner in need of grace. I didn't need to rededicate my life to trying harder. I needed a Savior. We prayed, and I had no doubt, then or since, that Jesus welcomed me into his heart. For the first time in my life I understood the lyrics and heard the music of the gospel. I felt so free, so clean, so connected with God. I found Steve and said, "I understand, I finally understand about your new friend!" It felt like I had inhaled a whole tank of helium. I danced on air! Many more dance lessons were to come.

What a paradox. Not until I truly felt guilty before God for my sin could I experience the depths of his love. What kept me from knowing the depth of my need? Is it really necessary to have a story of dissolute and despondent living to enter into the joy of salvation? Did I have to abuse alcohol and live foolishly in order to come to Jesus? Absolutely not! Many things keep us from the dance of the gospel. A part of my problem came from believing a gospel that was no gospel at all. For eighteen years I had been reading off of the wrong lyric sheet.

Believing the gospel is not like going to a frozen yogurt shop and picking out a flavor that satisfies your own particular taste buds from a menu of equally valid options. There are many false and incomplete gospels that keep us from understanding the gospel sooner. Here are a few common ones:

1. An Inadequate Understanding of Sin

When I was six, I stole a baseball from the Ben Franklin Dime Store. I felt guilty enough as I sneaked it into my hat, but I felt even worse when my parents discovered my larceny and made me return the ball to the store's owner, a neighbor and fellow church member. Fear gripped my heart as I knocked on her door. I prayed, "God, don't let Mrs. Dillahey be too mad at me."

Another time, I reluctantly gave a girlfriend an answer on an eighth-grade science exam. But I only felt really bad as I walked to the principal's office after someone saw my act of generosity and turned me in. I prayed, "God, please, get me out of this mess, and I promise not to screw up again." The principal happened to be my Uncle Wink. What would he say to my mom?

In both cases, I had asked God for relief—not for forgiveness. In fact, most of the people I grew up with didn't think of themselves as sinners in need of grace. We saw ourselves as basically good folk who only need occasional help from God, especially at times of crisis. My view of sin looked something like this: "We all make mistakes. None of us is perfect. God understands. I'll avoid doing 'unchristian' things the best I can while I try to do the 'right thing.'" I "believed" in Jesus (whatever that meant) and tried to do the "right things." To me, those two things were the essence of Christianity.

For me, prayer amounted to a superstitious ritual. I said the classic "Now-I-lay-me-down-to-sleep" prayer every night in about five seconds. I kept a Bible in the headboard of my bed like a rabbit's foot or a four-leaf clover. Though I never read the Bible, I feared ever placing *anything* on top of it. I had a horrid fear of "taking the Lord's name in vain," which simply meant never saying a certain curse word out loud. As a family we said grace at mealtime, but I never remember our having a single conversation about God.

So what would happen when I didn't do the "Christian thing"? Not much. Maybe a little bad luck, but everything would be okay in the end. I believed this way up till the very night I became a Christian. At no time, even during my wildest band days, did I think differently.

2. Sentimental Belief About Death

Every funeral I attended before becoming a Christian reinforced this way of thinking. No one really died, they just "passed on" or "left us for something better." Whatever the passion or hobby of the "departed" became the metaphor of the afterlife. "Good ol' Fred has joined the big foursome in the sky. He is probably carting around heaven's golf course with Gabriel, Jesus, and his best friend, Bill, who passed away last year." "Dear Nellie, how she loved to cook. Knowing her, she's probably in God's kitchen cooking for all the angels." Somewhere along the way I also got the idea that if a child died it was because God needed more little angels. It seemed like all you had to do to go to heaven is die! Sin, belief, and forgiveness did not really count for much.

3. A Missing Doctrine of Conversion

In the southern spiritual culture in which I grew up, you did not have to be "born again" to become a Christian. You simply had to be born in America. I remember hearing on Fourth of Julys and other patriotic holidays, "Be glad that you were born in a Christian nation." I assumed that meant all Americans are Christians unless they choose not to be. It saddens me to realize how much my image of God looked like Uncle Sam.

4. A Minimized View of God's Righteousness

Perhaps the root of all wrong gospels, including the one I believed, can be traced to unbiblical images of God. What is God like? This is the most important question we can ask. If our answer does not come from the Scripture, it will come from other sources, all of which vie for the right to define him. To be wrong about God's identity is to be wrong about everything, including who *we* are, what God expects of us, and how we can be in relationship with him.

Not only did I imagine God to be wearing red, white, and blue, I also believed him to be like a benign grandfatherly schoolteacher. He makes a lot of threats about grades and summer school, but at the end of every term he always applies a huge curve. No one has ever failed.

Then what *is* God like? According to the Bible he is absolutely holy. In fact, the only characteristic of God that is ever trebled in the Scriptures is his holiness. The angels in heaven cry out with affectionate reverence, "Day and night they never stop saying: 'Holy, holy, holy is the Lord God Almighty, who was, and is, and is to come'" (Rev. 4:8). To affirm that God is holy is to acknowledge that he is altogether "other" and distinct from us. He is dependent on nothing and no one.

God's holiness is also a revelation of his righteous character and of what he requires of us to be in a relationship with him. How great or minimal are these requirements? I had no idea, growing up, since I never read or studied the Bible. Most of my Sunday school teaching led me to believe that everything boiled down to making Jesus happy by "being good." Every Bible story ended up with a moral twist.

But when we read the Bible objectively, we soon realize that none of us can possibly meet what God requires of us in his law. It's like making Michael Jordan score 1000 points in one game, blindfolded, before he can get into the NBA Hall of Fame. It'll never happen. Why, then, did God give us the law if it is impossible to obey? Isn't this unfair? Quite the contrary! God's law drives us to Jesus as our only hope.

As I sat in the theater the night I became a Christian, I began to realize the enormity of my need. Otherwise, I could never have taken advantage of God's great provision in the gospel. The Holy Spirit convinced me that God's standard of judgment is his perfect righteousness, but before I could have a relationship with God and live with him forever in heaven, I had to be *perfect* like him, that's all, just *perfect!* But there's no way we can be as holy and righteous as God. Realizing this caused me to despair. "What hope do I have?" I asked myself.

But that night I also understood for the first time that Jesus fulfilled the law for me. He lived a perfect life of obedience on my behalf and died in my place, receiving on the cross the punishment that I deserved for breaking God's laws. When I put my trust in Jesus, God forgave all of my sins (past, present, and future) and declared me righteous in his sight. He put the righteousness of Jesus in my account that very night. Now *that* caused me to dance!

Great joy came to my heart when I realized that believing the gospel is like going to court to face your unpayable debt and your demanding creditors, knowing full well that you are legally guilty and totally bankrupt. When you drive into the parking lot of the courthouse, however, your attorney runs out to greet you, throwing confetti in the air and blowing a noisemaker. You fail to see the humor in your hour of greatest despair. "What kind of sick man is this?" you mutter to yourself.

"I have great news!" he shouts. "The president of the bank (who also happens to be the judge in this small town), has absorbed all of your debts and has established a perpetual account of unlimited funds to meet all of your needs! Friend, the only debt you have left is one of gratitude and love to the one who has been so gracious and generous with you!"

Amazing. God provides us with the righteousness that his own law demands. We receive his pardon and righteousness by faith, as a gift. We will never be more acceptable to God nor more beautiful to him than we are right now. It is on the basis of this righteousness, which we receive *passively,* that God accepts us, not on the basis of our own *active* righteousness. This righteousness is ours forever, and it is neither affected by our obedience nor by our disobedience. God cannot love us more than he does right now, and he will never love us any less. In fact, he loves us as much as he loves his own Son, Jesus!

The Heidelberg Catechism, written by a group of German Christians in the sixteenth century, summarizes this wonderful truth like this:

Q. How are you right with God?

A. Only by true faith in Jesus Christ. Even though my conscience accuses me of having grievously sinned against all God's commandments and of never having kept any of them, and even though I am still inclined toward all evil, nevertheless, without my deserving it at all, out of sheer grace, God grants and credits to me the perfect satisfaction, righteousness, and holiness of Christ, as if I had never sinned nor been a sinner, as if I had been perfectly obedient as Christ was obedient for me. All I need to do is accept this gift of God with a believing heart.[2]

Are *you* dancing yet?

Only in light of God's character and righteousness can we gain a proper diagnosis of our condition. If we minimize the demands of God's righteousness, we marginalize our need for his grace. This is the essence of all false gospels, and with false gospels we end up looking for a helper, not a Savior.

How Big Is Your Gospel?

It is both necessary and freeing, therefore, to have the proper diagnosis of our illness, even when we learn that our condition is a whole lot worse than we thought or hoped. I have a painfully memorable story to demonstrate this truth.

One hot summer day as a third grader, I went swimming with some buddies at our public pool. For some reason, I decided to try a back flip off of the side of the pool—never mind that I had never attempted such a feat. Crouching down, I sprang out, thrusting my head back and feet up, anticipating a perfect Olympic 10. The next thing I remember, I was floating facedown in chlorinated water, which was turning pink, with the blood gushing from my head. My head had struck the side of the pool.

A startled stranger fished me out of the water in my groggy and bloody state and sat me down beside the pool. I will never forget the pool manager's words as he stooped over me to examine my wound. He took one casual look at my gaping wound and said, "He'll be all right. Just put a bandage on him." His words comforted me so much. That's exactly what I wanted to hear. But, alas, my mom had a different idea. As soon as she arrived we headed straight for the emergency room.

The doctor wasted no time in sending me to an outpatient operating room. Lying on the gurney, I noticed a linen-covered tray a nurse placed right beside my head. I lifted up the sterile cloth and saw what looked like a foot-long syringe with a needle the size of a nail. Lying next to it was an assortment of other scary tools: pliers, wire clippers, forceps, and some strange-looking stringlike stuff. "Oh, no!" I cried. "Does this mean I'm going to have stitches?" I had always dreaded getting "sewn up" as a kid. My imagination ran wild after hearing some of my friends' "tales of the catgut." I cried and cried. Couldn't the pool manager be right? Why not just put a big bandage on the hole in my head? One hour, six shots, and twenty-three double stitches later, I went home.

In Jeremiah's day God rebuked the prophets and priests who dressed "the wound of my people as though it were not serious. 'Peace, peace,' they say when there is no peace" (Jer. 8:11). I could have died from infection without the proper care for my wounded head. I could have died eternally without the proper care for my sinful heart. Only those who have been exposed by the law can have any hope of rejoicing in the Son.

If someone has been taught that all he needs is a Donald Duck inner tube instead of mouth-to-mouth resuscitation to be rescued from drowning in sin, then what's the big deal? Just blow up your little floatie, put it on, and get on with life. But it is only the "gospel of God's grace" that can meet our great need. The wrong lyric will always lead to the wrong music or to no music at all. So what does this gospel dance look like?

Parables of Joy

Even though our journeys differ at some points, my story resembles that of the Prodigal Son (Luke 15). God wants us to know the almost unimaginable joy *he* experiences when we come home from any of the many distant countries we run to in our sin, pain, and foolishness. It is the joy of God that liberates our hearts to dance.

The legalists of Jesus' day, the Pharisees and teachers of the law, continued to despise him for welcoming "sinners and tax collectors" so readily. One day while both Pharisees and a large crowd of these "sinners" gathered around to hear him, Jesus described a chapter in the life of a wealthy family in the Middle East, an estate that required "many hired men" to shoulder all the work. The patriarch had two sons. The younger, for whatever reason, decided that life in his father's house simply wasn't enough. We can only speculate about his reasons for wanting to leave. Was it youthful wanderlust, boredom, immaturity, a conflict at home? Had he outgrown the need for a dad? We don't know. What causes *any* of us to look elsewhere beyond God for life?

Impudently, the younger son insisted that his father give him his portion of his inheritance legally due at the time of his dad's death. "Father, give me my share of the estate." The implication of such a demand being, "Father, I wish you were already dead."

Though he had reason and authority to deny such a request, and to cut his arrogant son out of his will alltogether, the father divided his estate between his boys. The younger son received a third of the estate, while his older brother, the firstborn, received two-thirds. Why did the father concede? Did he simply cave in to his son's demand because of weakness? Or is this father a lot wiser than we assume?

The younger brother "got together all he had," apparently planning never to return, and left for "a distant country." Did he know where he was going when he pulled away from home? Maybe, maybe not. Any distant country would have provided a suitable address given the restlessness of his soul. An intense longing and demand for autonomy and "freedom" will lead us anywhere away from whatever home is confining us.

When he arrived in that faraway land, the sights, smells, and sounds probably offered an immediate sense of relief and confirmation that "*this* is now my home." A man or woman with money is never a stranger for long. New friends, partying, no responsibility, what more could he want? There is pleasure in sin—for a season. The narcotic of change and the illusion of being in control offer instant, but short-lived, relief.

Jesus simply said that in that country he began to "squander his wealth in wild living." How long does the "good life" last? Usually as long as your pockets are deep. It really doesn't take long to go through a third of an estate, even if it's a big estate.

Seasons change, and, in God's mercy, it's never far from pride to brokenness—it just takes a while to get there. Jesus describes a famine that came to that country, just like the famine that came into the prodigal's heart. His financial resources gave out, and finally, "he began to be in need." Surely those who had shared in his good fortune and generosity would help him in his hour of adversity. "I'll call my friends. We'll get through this season together." But those who were so ready to spend his inheritance were busy looking for their own next free lunch.

How humbling. He had to find some kind of job just to survive. For a brief season he had been top dog in that country, the king of his own little world. Now he was reduced to living as a hired man, a servant, a common laborer working in the field feeding pigs. In Jewish culture, such work was not simply dirty, it was ceremonially forbidden. He was unclean. But desperate men resort to desperate measures.

How hungry is hungry? At the time when even the pig food started looking good, "he came to his senses." Memories of life in his father's house began to fill his starving soul. As Jesus tells the story, we quickly realize that this is no mere tale of pragmatism and survival. This young man is not just thinking about how he can keep from dying. There is a larger and grander thing going on inside of him. He isn't just hungry for food, he is hungry for home. Sitting in the consequences of his foolish choices, his attention turns from a starving belly to a starving heart.

"What have I done? What was I thinking? There is abundance in my father's house, and I'm sitting here. . . . My father . . . I have sinned against God and him. I'm not even worthy to refer to him as my father anymore. Perhaps he would let me become one of his servants if I go back home. Why did I ever leave?" What we do in the midst of such shameful awareness is the clearest indication of the depths of our hunger and thirst. Jesus comments, "So he got up and went to his father."

How long does it take for a broken and shamed son to come home from a distant country? I've often tried to imagine what the scene looked like when he left home with a light heart and so many possessions. Did it take a team of burros and a cart to carry all his stuff? Did he have camels to get him to his destination as fast as possible? Now, he walks on foot slowly carrying a heart heavy laden with guilt and a mind cramping with painful doubts about the reception that awaits him. How many times did he rewrite and rehearse the first words he would say to his father? What a stark contrast!

Jesus surprises us—no, he shocks us—with what comes next. While this young son, who had probably aged considerably in recent months, was still "a long way off," his father saw him coming. What are we to imagine? Did the father just happen to be looking out the window or over the wall at the right time? Or had one of his servants seen the disheveled son coming and then rushed home to tell the father? We don't know. But clearly the impression Jesus gives is that this father's heart had been praying and longing for this day ever since his son left.

Hiking up the long skirt of his robe he ran toward his son with shameless abandon. "*Filled* with compassion," he threw his out-stretched arms around his boy and began to lavish him with many kisses.

What must the son have felt? "Does my father really know who he's kissing? Perhaps he has me confused with someone else." He begins his well-rehearsed speech of humiliation. "Father, I have sinned . . ."

But there is no mistaken identity. "Welcome home, son. I have missed you. Quick, my good servants! Fetch the best robe in my closet, my signet ring, and a new pair of sandals. This son of mine was as good as dead. Look! He is alive again. He's home. Let's have a party!" A fattened calf was barbecued on his behalf, and feasting with celebration broke out as spirited sounds of music and merrymaking filled the house. What an astonishing scene, scandalous to many, especially to the religious legalists hearing this story!

The son, exhausted from the toll of his long journey, attempts to drink all of this in. As he makes his way into the same dining room he had eaten in for so many years, now alive with feasting on *his* behalf, he continues to struggle with disbelief. "Am I dreaming? Maybe I'm hallucinating. I know, it's a mirage. I'm still lost in the desert somewhere."

Perhaps the next scene looked something like this. The father comes and takes his son's hand, beckoning him to join the dance. The father himself is rejoicing and singing with the other guests as together they share the blessedness of the moment as they enjoy the spirited sounds of the musicians. The stunned son has heard these same words and melodies before, but never like this. The music seems so new. Shoulder to shoulder with his father, he can't help but wonder to him-self as they enjoy the dances that have always been a part of the community, "What is so different? There's a light in my father's eye and a warmth in his embrace that I've never noticed till now. Though I deserve his disdain, I feel his delight. How can this be?" They partied late into the night. This wouldn't be the last of the dancing, however.

A God Who Delights in His Children

Some would suggest that it is hyperbole to infer that God rejoices like this over his children. But ponder this great promise of the Scriptures: "The LORD your God is with you, he is mighty to save. He will take great delight in you, he will quiet you with his love, he will rejoice over you with singing" (Zeph. 3:17). This verse is ours to believe and appropriate because of what Jesus has accomplished through his life and death on our behalf.

In Zephaniah 3:14–15 we read: "Sing, O Daughter of Zion; shout aloud, O Israel! Be glad and rejoice with all your heart, O Daughter of Jerusalem! The LORD has taken away your punishment, he has turned back your enemy. The LORD, the King of Israel, is with you; never again will you fear any harm." God rejoices, and we rejoice because Jesus has accomplished everything necessary for our salvation. Jesus has taken away our punishment on the cross. There he defeated our great enemy, Satan.

God's loudest singing and his most passionate delight is expressed in the gospel of his grace. Through the gospel God is with us. By the gospel he saves us. In the gospel he delights in us. Through the gospel he quiets us with his love. In the gospel we hear him rejoice over us with singing! Does your heart allow you to imagine God himself serenading you with his own love songs?

The same delight that God has in his only begotten Son, he has for his adopted sons and daughters (Matt. 12:18)! Because of the gospel, God loves us as much as he loves Jesus! With speechless wonder we should respond to such a truth, and then get up and start dancing!

John Owen, the great English Puritan theologian wrote: "The greatest sorrow and burden you can lay on the Father, the greatest unkindness you can do to him is not to believe that he loves you."[3] To the degree that we live with a convinced awareness of God's love for us in Christ, to that degree will we love him with everything that we have and are.

Who Gets to Dance?

Who, then, hears the music of the gospel? When does the dance begin? Every time the Spirit applies the law of God to our consciences in a way that moves us to repentant faith, to boasting in Jesus rather than ourselves, the gospel band strikes up, angels sing, and the Father rejoices. "There is more rejoicing in heaven over one sinner who repents than over ninety-nine righteous persons who do not need to repent" (Luke 15:7).

In the first of his Ninety-five Theses nailed to the door at Wittenberg, Martin Luther declared that "repentance is a way of life" and not merely the act by which we initially become believers. It is a way of life defined by the gospel and empowered by God's Spirit. As Christians, we need the gospel just as much as non-Christians do. The same grace that establishes our relationship with God also brings us to maturity.

Just as I needed to know the depth of my need to enter into the riches of God's provision in the gospel, so this younger of two brothers also needed to experience the dark condition of his heart to enjoy the fullness of his father's delight. Neither my pilgrimage into the land of "beach music" nor his foray to a "distant country" made us more worthy of God's judgment. These trips simply exposed our foolish and sinful hearts, revealing what was always there.

The younger son needed to know that God comes like a hurricane wind, exposing and tearing down one's idols and illusions, before the gentle, calming breeze of forgiveness can be experienced.

God's law is meant to drive us to Christ, not to another Christian self-help course. The true gospel is not a harmless zephyr of personal affirmation. Jesus did not die simply to rescue us from a poor self-image; rather, God is committed to transforming each of us into the perfect likeness of Jesus, a process that will only be finished in heaven.

Take Off the Grave Clothes and Let Him Go

In the gospel, we *continue* to discover that our need for a changed heart is far greater than we ever imagined, but God is gracious with us. His timetable for our growth is an expression of his fatherly wisdom and relentless tenderness. His plan is to humble us, not humiliate us—to free us to know more of his love and to become more like Jesus, not to place us back into the slavery of shame and self-contempt.

I have often thought of the time when Jesus raised his friend Lazarus from the dead as a helpful metaphor of the process of growing in grace. As Lazarus came forth from the tomb, "the dead man came out, his hands and feet wrapped with strips of linen, and a cloth around his face. Jesus said to them, 'Take off the grave clothes and let him go'" (John 11:43–44).

It is helpful to think of a Christian as someone who has been raised from spiritual death in Christ and called forth to a life of freedom and transformation. When we first come alive in Christ we are still bound with many "grave clothes." These grave clothes represent whatever keeps us from loving God with all of our heart and loving each other as God loves us.

Spiritual growth involves identifying and removing these grave clothes so that we may freely love. A young believer doesn't perceive just how many layers there are. A maturing believer realizes that not just his hands and his feet and eyes but also his mind and his heart are bound and need the healing and liberating work of God's grace. Perhaps it's a good thing that Lazarus' friends did not hold up a mirror to him as soon as he came out from the grave! As young believers, we would be devastated if our Father were to reveal to us too early the whole panorama of his planned work in our lives. To see clearly the full contrast between what our hearts are *really* like and what the heart of Jesus is like would overwhelm us to the point of despair.

This is why it is so important to be rooted in the grace of the gospel and the love of God. It is only those who know themselves to be already pardoned and declared righteous by faith in Jesus who can submit with confidence and joy to the painfully good process of having their grave clothes exposed and removed. It is they who can affirm, even with tears in their eyes and pain in their hearts, "My Father will bring to completion the good work he has begun in me" (Phil. 1:6).

Prone to Wander, Not Wonder

A sign of maturity is to recognize that our own hearts are idol factories until we are made perfect in Jesus. Henri Nouwen speaks for all of us when he says,

> I leave home every time I lose faith in the voice that calls me the Beloved and follow the voices that offer a great variety of ways to win the love I so much desire. As long as I keep looking for my true self in the world of conditional love, I will remain "hooked" to the world—trying, failing, and trying again. It is a world that fosters addictions because what it offers cannot satisfy the deepest craving of my heart.[4]

As we grow in Christ, we discover how we worship approval, the security of a 401(k), the safety of our own ingrown Christian community, and other creature comforts, much more than we worship God. As Kierkegaard wrote in *Sickness Unto Death*, most of us would rather "tranquilize ourselves with the trivial."[5]

But as the Holy Spirit begins to convicts us, we come to our senses, run home to our Father, receive more grace and dance with him the dance of hearts set free. For in the gospel we also know ourselves to be more loved than we ever hoped or dreamed. The Father continues to wait and to pursue, longing to be gracious to *you*.

chapter three

[HOPE FOR RETURNING PRODIGALS AND RECOVERING PHARISEES]

The Change

Well I got myself a T-shirt that says what I believe
I got letters on my bracelet to serve as my ID
I got the necklace and the key chain
And almost everything a good Christian needs, yeah
I got the little Bible magnets on my refrigerator door
And a welcome mat to bless you before you walk across
my floor
I got a Jesus bumper sticker
And the outline of a fish stuck on my car
And even though this stuff's all well and good, yeah
I cannot help but ask myself—

What about the change
What about the difference
What about the grace
What about forgiveness
What about a life that's showing
I'm undergoing the change, yeah
I'm undergoing the change
Well I've got this way of thinking that comes so
naturally
Where I believe the whole world is revolving around me
And I got this way of living that I have to die to every
single day
'Cause if God's Spirit lives inside of me, yeah
I'm gonna live life differently

I'm gonna have the change
I'm gonna have the difference
I'm gonna have the grace
I'm gonna have forgiveness
I'm gonna live a life that's showing
I'm undergoing the change

What about the change
What about the difference
What about the grace
What about forgiveness
I want to live a life that's showing
I'm undergoing the change

Steven:

I'm a born performer. I was even conceived with a role to play. My parents had struggled in their relationship and had considered separation. One night, as they discussed their options, they wondered if having another child might ease the pain that had defined their marriage. My brother, Herbie, had brought them a reason to stay together. Perhaps the same bonding could occur again. Later, however, their marriage failed anyway.

So on November 2, 1962, I rode in on my white horse to save the day. Actually, I came in kicking and screaming and destroying diapers, but the white horse image seems to define the expectation placed upon me. Early in life, I sensed a need to come through for those around me, and I didn't want to disappoint anyone. Pull up the curtain and let the entertainment begin! It didn't take long for me to develop a passion for a great performance and a distaste, if not disdain, for a bad one.

As a father of two Little Leaguers of my own, I am reminded of the emotional trauma of the strikeout and the elation of the homer! To a young boy, those two expressions facilitate the greatest contrast in emotions imaginable, and when they come in the same game, it's almost too much to take! As an outfielder for the Concord Lions, I had my first taste of the "thrill of victory and the agony of defeat," as they used to say on ABC's *Wide World of Sports*.

I stood at the plate, knocking off the imaginary mud from my rubber cleats. Staring down the three-and-a-half-foot-tall pitcher standing on the mound forty-five feet away, I got low in my stance, preparing to knock that little sphere of cork and cowhide clear into the next county. Within what seemed like milliseconds, I heard the umpire utter that shame-producing phrase, "Strike three! You're out." I walked the three miles, or so it seemed, back to the dugout, fighting back the tears until I reached the bench. There the tears won and I broke down. I got the obligatory "that's-okay-you'll-get-'em-next-time" pat on the back from my teammates as I wallowed in my failure.

Eight batters later, I could almost hear the "oh no, it's him again" sighs as I stepped up to bat. Once again, I got in my stance. I don't remember the count, but I do remember swinging the bat, watching the ball disappear into the outfield, and running like there would be no tomorrow. Like a scene from *Field of Dreams,* I stepped on home plate and heard the cheering crowd.

At that very moment, something was born inside me. It felt good to deliver, to come through for my team. Without realizing it, I determined from that point on to go for a home run every time I swung a bat. I wanted to perform—and perform well. The rush I got from the crowd's applause and my teammates' approval pushed a button and threw a lever deep in my gut. Though I never hit another homer, I began to look for other playing fields where "home-run" performances could be achieved. Music had already emerged as a prime contender.

I started performing publicly as a wee first grader. Every October our elementary school had a Fall Festival, which culminated in a much-anticipated talent show. Each fall, my brother and I, known naturally as the "Chapman Brothers," were expected to showcase our budding skills in this community-wide talentfest. In third grade, however, the unthinkable occurred. Just as Herbie and I were getting ready for our annual dazzling demonstration of Broadway-bound talent, I came down with the flu. Devastation! I managed to get to the auditorium and find a place to lie down backstage, with a trash can by my side, trying to keep my Coke and aspirin down. Still holding out for a miracle, it killed me to hear the announcer say to the primed and excited audience, "Due to an illness, the Chapman Brothers will not be able to perform."

Like a magic elixir, the groans of disappointment from the crowd brought a renewed strength to my whole eight-year-old frame. "The show must go on!" I said to myself. After a few other acts, the Chapman Brothers were announced and greeted with spirited cheers of approval. Herbie and I performed an adrenaline-injected version of Donny Osmond's "Go Away Little Girl," and the crowd awarded our rendering of this teenybopper classic with a Beatles-like ovation. We hit a "home run," and it felt good. My dad and mom were proud. Maybe I could salvage their marriage after all.

In this way, I allowed myself to get pulled right into the pressure cooker of being a "fixer." Little did I realize how easy it would be to take this performance-based living right into my relationship with God.

As I've already shared, the story of my coming to faith in Christ does not include deep, dark, sordid tales of life in the gutter or recovering from drug addiction. The so-called Technicolor sins were not the ones I have had to overcome, though I know myself capable of committing any sin. I've always been a pretty well-behaved fair-haired Kentucky boy. But ever so imperceptibly, I began to grow the heart of a legalist, discovering that the same applause garnered from hitting home runs and making music could be found by being a "good boy." Naturally, I believed God liked me better when I obeyed him and that he might cause me to have a flat tire, or some other discomfort, if I disobeyed him.

The problem with legalism, of course, is that it leads to Pharisaism. The Pharisee's relating style looks something like this: If *I* have to perform well, then *you* have to perform well too. Your bad performance is going to cost me, so you better not fail. I'll reward you if you do good, and I'll punish you if you disappoint me.

The longer you live as a Pharisee, of course, the less you make of your own failures—and the more you exaggerate those of others. I've seen this pattern in my family (how I react to my children's foibles and "strikeouts"), in my band (expecting the performance of my dreams every time we get onstage), in the culture (thanking God that I'm not like those people who do all of the really dastardly evil stuff).

Legalism is an ugly and destructive disease. It destroys both the carrier and those around him or her. This cancer and its effects are seen so clearly in the graceless heart of the elder brother in Luke 15. He is an example of a believer who seems to be, if it were possible, allergic to God's love.

What's the cure? The more I expose my heart to the gospel of God's grace, the more offended I am by my own pharisaical heart and the more I long to have a grace-saturated heart. Only God's love can melt the heart of a legalist. The only applause worth living for is that which we freely get in the gospel of God's grace. Jesus has won the applause of heaven for us. No, I've never had to go to Betty Ford's to recover from a chemical addiction. But I do have to go to Jesus and his grace to help me recover from my legalism and Pharisaism.

I invite you to take a fresh look at the story of the other lost son. Perhaps you're a lot more like me and Scotty than you realize!

Scotty:

Two Lost Sons—The Story of the Other Prodigal

We usually call Jesus' story in Luke 15:11–32 "The Parable of the Prodigal Son." But there are *two* lost sons in the story, both of whom are loved and pursued by the compassionate father, though only one of them is found. Both are invited to the party and encouraged to join the dance, but only one responds. What made it so easy for the older brother to reject this gracious invitation?

Let me tell you the other half of the story.

The Other Prodigal Son

The older son, as usual, had been hard at work in the field. From early in the morning to late at night, you could find him there, being the responsible overseer of his father's estate. He cared about his father's interests, for in time, they would be his. Supervising the servants, guarding the grounds, considering ways to increase the harvest—no one ever charged him with being a sluggard!

Things hadn't changed that much since his younger brother had left. His father seemed sad, but there wasn't any drop-off in production. It didn't surprise him at all when the "lazy party boy" decided to take off. *Good riddance,* he thought the day his brother left. They never were very close. The younger brother had never really contributed to the family business anyway.

One day, while returning from the field, the older brother heard a vaguely familiar sound coming from his own house. He was puzzled, not because he had never heard it before but because it had been so long since the joy of music and dancing filled the corridors of *his* house.

Intrigued and perplexed, he called for one of the servants, who reported with great enthusiasm, "Your little brother! He's back! Your father had us kill the calf he's been fattening, and he told us to get all the neighbors and friends together for a big party. I don't remember when I have seen your father so happy. He's dancing around like a child! Come and see for yourself!"

The last thing the elder brother wanted to fill his eyes with was the sight of his father acting silly over the return of his good-for-nothing younger brother. So the older brother became angry and refused the servant's plea to join the celebration. That same servant told the father, "Your older son is in the courtyard. I told him our good news, but he refuses to join us."

The loving father went out and pleaded with him: "Come and see your brother! It's a miracle! What I've longed for all these days has finally happened. Come in, son, and rejoice with us!"

With the same ugly attitude the younger son had shown to his father when he demanded his inheritance, the older son spoke: "Look! All these years I've been your slave. I've never disobeyed your orders. What have you ever given me? Not even a young goat that I could share with *my* friends! And now, this son of yours—he's no brother of mine—he comes back after wasting the money I helped you earn—spending it on who knows what, including prostitutes no doubt—and what do you do? You kill the fattened calf and act like everything's okay. I don't get it, Father, I don't get it! How can you let him get away with everything he's done to us?"

In an amazing display of composure, mercy, and compassion, the father responded, "My son, you are always with me. We work together, we pray together, we struggle together. We're a family. Everything that I have is yours. Can't you understand what's happened? We have no other choice but to celebrate and rejoice. Your brother—and he's your brother even though you have never been close—was dead; he was lost, and now we have him back!"

The Unrighteousness of Self-righteousness

While the younger brother had lived as a stranger *to* his family, the older brother lived like a stranger *in* his family. He lived in his own house as a self-righteous orphan. When his father said, "You are always with me," it wasn't because the son never left his father's side, but because the father always kept him in his heart.

He was an heir of great riches; in fact as the oldest son, no one had a greater legal claim on the father's estate than he did, and yet he lived with a bankrupt soul. The pleading of the father for the elder brother to come inside and enjoy the feasting and dancing is music more grand and loud than that which echoes from the house. Sadly, he is alive to neither. How are we to understand his graceless heart?

He is like the man who just flew to Paris aboard the Concorde on an all-expense-paid vacation, who complained throughout the flight about the movie and food, and then bemoans the fact that the plane landed fifteen minutes late! Or the older brother is like the woman who received a magnificent three-carat-diamond engagement ring but is irritated that it didn't come with flowers and wine. Or the child who after opening twenty-seven Christmas presents asks, "Is that all?"

Some believers make you want to shake them and say, "What *is* your problem? Wake up! Don't you realize what you have?" But perhaps *we* are the ones who need to be shaken. It's possible that the elder brother's problem is my problem and yours. As a pastor for over twenty years, I can say with no hesitation that for every younger brother I encounter in ministry, I meet five elder brothers. The elder-brother syndrome is epidemic in the body of Christ. Too many Christians live as though heaven is a gift, but the rest of the Christian life is kind of a "church purgatory"!

It is all too common for Christians to be lost in the Father's house; to be in his family but a stranger to his affections; to be heir of his whole estate and yet living impoverished lives bereft of the riches of his grace; to vaguely hear the music and the dancing of the Father's celebrations and yet to despise the very sound. The younger son could not experience the grandeur of his father's love until he realized the depth of his own unrighteousness. So too the older son can't move out of the orphanage of his hard heart onto the dance floor of his father's delight until he sees the ugliness of his self-righteousness. I know of no evil with greater power to rob a heart of grace and destroy a man, a marriage, a family, a church, a community, a nation than self-righteousness and its wellspring—legalism.

In reality, it is easier to be convinced of our unrighteousness than our self-righteousness. Unrighteousness is usually in direct opposition to Scripture or conscience; it is external, observable, and usually easy to define. But self-righteousness is more subtle. Most self-righteous people are religious. They have strong passions about certain rules and regulations. When the self-righteous encounter the irreligious or those who "break the rules," they feel good about themselves and condescending toward the lawbreakers. This is the attitude of the older brother to his younger brother. It is also an attitude I have battled throughout much of my Christian life.

The truth is, there is no greater unrighteousness than self-righteousness. Jesus' most scathing remarks were directed not at pagans and "sinners," but at condescending religious people, blind to their own graceless hearts. Jesus singled out the scribes and Pharisees as the worst examples of this evil. They were the religious leaders who taught that God's acceptance of us is based on our scrupulous adherence to the laws of Moses. Typically, they were confident of their own righteousness but suspect of everyone else's. Thus, Pharisaism emerged as a term synonymous with self-righteousness.

The Root of Pharisaism Is Legalism

Legalism teaches: "I can *merit* forgiveness and acceptance by God through religious duty and obedience to his commandments." It teaches: "I must *maintain* forgiveness and acceptance by God through religious duty and obedience to his commandments."

Legalism is not just sub-Christian or non-Christian. It is anti-Christian.

The Fruit of Pharisaism Is Self-righteousness and/or an Orphan Spirit

Self-righteousness is the proud, judgmental attitude born out of the false gospel of legalism. The self-righteous individual puts his confidence in what he has done to earn God's favor.

An *orphan spirit* is the self-centered attitude of a believer who lives either ignorant *of* or indifferent *to* the fact that God is his or her Abba, Father. Rose Marie Miller describes the characteristics of a Christian orphan in her book, *From Fear to Freedom*.

> Life consciously or unconsciously is centered on personal autonomy and moral willpower, with grace understood as God's maintaining your own strength—not as his transforming power.
>
> Faith is defined as trying harder to do and be better, with a view to establishing a good record leading to self-justification.
>
> Obedience is related to external, visible duties, with attitudes and deeper motivation virtually ignored.
>
> "What people think" is represented as the real moral standard, based upon visible success and failure.
>
> An *I-am-a-victim* attitude is supported by coping strategies: wall building, blame shifting, gossiping, and defending. All this is accompanied by intense feelings of aloneness, believing that no one understands and that one is trapped by circumstances.[1]

You're Not Legalistic Enough!

Oddly, the legalist's main error is that none of them are legalistic enough! They all lower the demands of the law for themselves so that they are doable. They do this by focusing more on rules to be kept rather than relationships to be cultivated and people to be cared for. They are more preoccupied with laws to be obeyed rather than with love to be manifested. In so doing, they minimize the demands of the law because love, God's love, is the fulfillment of the law. It is always much easier to perform a task dutifully than it is to love, serve, and forgive someone from the heart. The way of grace is far messier than the way of law. Other-centered love is always more costly than self-centered piety.

For instance, the legalists of Jesus' day were more concerned about scrupulously observing the specifics of the Sabbath ordinance than they were in pondering the purpose why God even instituted Sabbath rest. The truth is, they turned a day of rest into a day of restlessness by heaping requirements on believers that God himself never commanded—such as how much weight could be lifted and how many steps one could walk before someone could legally be charged with breaking the Sabbath!

They completely missed the intent and spirit of the law. The apostle Paul writes, "The entire law is summed up in a single command: 'Love your neighbor as yourself'" (Gal. 5:14)—which apparently includes loving one's sheep as well, if it should fall into a pit on the Sabbath (Matt. 12:11–12). Such a legalistic attitude led Jesus to affirm, "The Sabbath was made for man, not man for the Sabbath" (Mk. 2:27). God instituted the Sabbath as a good gift to man, a principle of rest and reflection, not of rigorism and ritual. Our hearts are to draw near to God and to one another on the Sabbath as we live as good stewards of all things, including our schedules.

The legalist's distortion of God's law is graphically pointed out in the Sermon on the Mount, when Jesus boldly declares, "I tell you that unless your righteousness surpasses that of the Pharisees and the teachers of the law, you will certainly not enter the kingdom of heaven" (Matt. 5:20). In denouncing pharisaical self-righteousness, Jesus makes clear that the law is not just concerned with a doable, external conformity to its precepts. No, the law requires that I do the right thing perfectly and with a good heart. The law does not merely condemn murder but also anger (Matt. 5:21–22). It does not merely forbid having sex with someone who is not your spouse, it also forbids lust (Matt. 5:27–28).

One time a Pharisee asked Jesus, "'Teacher, which is the greatest commandment in the Law?' Jesus replied: "Love the Lord your God with all your heart and with all your soul and with all your mind." This is the first and greatest commandment. And the second is like it: "Love your neighbor as yourself." All the Law and the Prophets hang on these two commandments'" (Matt. 22:36–40).

How good is good enough? What does the law *really* require of us? All we need to do in order to earn our salvation is to love God and man with everything that we have and are, all the time and with a perfect attitude!

How foolish we are to presume that we ever have or could obey God in this fashion. With great poignancy Paul affirms this: "All who rely on observing the law are under a curse, for it is written: 'Cursed is everyone who does not continue to do everything written in the Book of the Law.' Clearly no one is justified before God by the law" (Gal. 3:10–11).

Even Our Righteousness Is Unrighteous

Martin Luther taught his followers to repent of both their unholy *and* good deeds alike. Luther understood that even our so-called "righteousness" is full of vanity and devoid of true godliness. Even our most selfless and sacrificial acts are shot through with sin. This is surely what the prophet Isaiah meant when he said, "All our righteous acts are like filthy rags" (Isa. 64:6); they are soiled and stained with the duplicity and self-serving motives of our hearts. They have no value in earning our salvation.

Jerry Bridges addresses the error of the Christian Pharisee in this way: "Your worst days are never so bad that you are beyond the *reach* of God's grace. And your best days are never so good that you are beyond the *need* of God's grace."[2]

The older brother was so near, yet so far away—so "right," but so wrong. He stood on the premises of grace, but was a stranger to its promises. So much of his behavior seemed so commendable. He was hardworking and obedient. But he had the heart of a graceless beast.

Until we learn to identify and despise our self-righteousness, we remain strangers to the music and the dance of the gospel. The *only* righteousness that meets God's requirement is the righteousness of Jesus, and the *only* way we receive this righteousness is *by grace through faith*.

My Life as a Christian Pharisee

I wish I could say that after my prodigal season of outward unrighteousness, like that of the younger brother, that I began walking in the responsible freedom of the gospel. The truth is I went to the opposite end of the spectrum and became as self-righteous as the older brother. I've been both a prodigal and a Pharisee, and I am no less capable of falling into either graceless pattern today. Our stories have the power to remind each of us not to think of ourselves more highly than we ought. For at any time we can flee the gospel of God's grace for some other gospel that is not a gospel at all.

I will never forget one particularly painful episode in my life— one that reveals the kind of arrogant self-righteousness I am capable of. I had just graduated from Westminster Theological Seminary. I had received as fine a theological training as anyone could have hoped for. Studying the doctrines of grace became a passion and a joy.

Both native Tarheels, my wife and I were excited when I got a call to join the staff of an outstanding church in Winston-Salem, North Carolina. They offered me the job of youth pastor, overseeing the nurture of junior and senior high students. This renewal-based fellowship happened to be the mainstream denomination in which I grew up. We were thrilled to move back home close to family and to have the opportunity to serve this thriving downtown church.

I was invited to attend a special retreat welcoming me to the staff, to be held in the beautiful mountains of western North Carolina. Seven of us attended—four pastors, the director of children's ministries, the director of worship ministries, and the business manager.

After an incredible meal, seasoned with lighthearted table banter, we settled in for an evening of getting to know the new kid on the staff—namely me! I was dessert. Then the senior pastor asked me, "So Scotty, what personal issues are you struggling with at this season in your life?"

Without blinking an eye, I responded confidently, "I don't have any questions left for which the Bible does not give me sufficient answers, and since I discovered the sovereignty of God, I don't struggle with anything."

Boom! There it was, the heart of a young Pharisee served up as the last course of a great supper. It was like going from prime rib to prime fool. Pharisees have answers for everything. They confuse knowledge with spirituality.

Their initial response was gracious. Yet, I could see it in their eyes, "We have just hired a pompous young idiot." How right they were! That night, instead of building a bridge into their hearts, I laid the foundation for a wall between us that got higher as I added one judgmental stone at a time.

For the better part of two years, I unwittingly became the self-appointed prosecuting attorney in that part of the body of Christ. With legal pad in heart, if not in hand, I took it upon myself to critique every sermon preached, every idea expressed, and every musical arrangement performed. How many times I thought to myself, *If they'd only listen to me, I could really turn things around here. I'd straighten out the theology, restructure the worship service, and get rid of some of those liberal deacons and elders.* How it pains me to document such immaturity and impertinence!

I wish I could blame it all on my seminary. Being a victim with an excuse is so much more fun than being an abuser without one. But the problem wasn't seminary. I had mastered the theology of grace without being mastered by the grace of that theology! I could spot bibli-cal and theological inconsistency a mile away, but I could not see the ungrace in my own heart.

So what happened? Eventually, one of my few close friends in that church got through to me. She was courageous enough to say, "Scotty, you're a tremendous teacher, but you have a hard time loving people. I know you're better than that." Those words, offered in such a gen-tle way by someone I trusted, had the effect of a hurricane. I was blown away. Her words cut with a precision and power I could not withstand. This devastating revelation was a gift of God's severe grace.

Like the Wizard of Oz, I had hidden behind my curtains of bib-lical and theological information. From there I could pretend to be big and powerful, projecting an image that was illusion, not reality. When my friend mercifully threw open the curtains and exposed me, it hurt, but it hurt redemptively. The Scriptures teach, "Faithful are the wounds of a friend" (Prov. 27:6 KJV). Through the pain of that moment I received an invitation to take a look at my proud heart and to consider why I have a hard time loving people who see things dif-ferently than me.

Why Do We Love So Little?

After that, I started to see myself in many of Jesus' stories about Phar-isees. The story of Simon, recorded in Luke 7, is a great example, in which another self-righteous man is exposed at a dinner gathering. Apparently, Simon had been intrigued by what he heard and saw of Jesus. So he invited the popular and controversial rabbi to his home to share a meal.

While Jesus and Simon were reclining at the table, an uninvited woman, identified to us only as one who had "lived a sinful life," came into the house. It was customary for the poor to be permitted to sit against the walls in the home of wealthier citizens during mealtime. The leftovers would be shared with them. But as a "public sinner," perhaps a prostitute, she would not be welcome. It took a tremen-dous amount of courage for her to come, especially into a Pharisee's home. She came, however, not to get food but to show her love.

Someone told her she would find Jesus here. Instead of sitting against the wall, she moved quietly toward Jesus and, kneeling at his extended feet, she began to weep and wet his feet with her salty tears. Wiping his feet with her long tresses, she proceeded to kiss his feet and pour perfume on them. Simon was incensed that such a woman was received so freely by his dinner guest. He seized the moment to render judgment against Jesus. "If this man were a prophet, he would know who is touching him and what kind of woman she is—that she is a sinner." Pharisaism is always on the outlook to confirm its critical prejudices.

Jesus knew exactly what was going on. He told Simon a parable about two borrowers and a moneylender. "There were two men who owed money to the same lender. One owed five hundred days' worth of wages and the other owed fifty days' worth. Neither had the means to repay their debt. But the moneylender did the unexpected. He canceled both debts. Simon, which of these two men do you suppose will love the moneylender more?"

Simon equivocates: "I suppose the one who had the bigger debt canceled." What's to suppose? This isn't quantum physics or graduate level mathematics! It's a simple equation of grace. Maybe that's why it was so hard for the well-trained Pharisee to understand. He never took that course. In fact, grace was nowhere in the curriculum of the school from which he graduated.

To make sure that Simon got the point, Jesus drew attention to the startling contrast between the Pharisee's lack of common courtesy toward his dinner guest and the courageous and costly love this woman had shown Jesus. "Do you see this woman?" Jesus asked. But Simon didn't really see her at all. In fact he had a hard time seeing anything after she began to linger at Jesus' feet. He saw only a "sinful woman" whose action, measured by his religious legalism and censorious heart, disgusted him.

One of the ugliest aspects of legalism is its power to render people invisible. People are not seen as image bearers of God who are to be known, understood, and loved, even when they fail miserably. They are simply pluses or minuses in the ledger of life. The Pharisee has little time to waste on listening to a person's story. All of life is reduced to successes and failures. Legalism reduces people to nonperson status.

While Simon, as the host, had not even extended the common social courtesies to Jesus, the woman, however, had been profuse in her expressions of welcome and respect. But this story is not about dinner parties and good manners, but rather about forgiveness and overflowing love.

Somewhere, before this meeting in Simon's home, this woman had experienced the grace that Jesus pours out abundantly on those who admit their sinful condition. Perhaps she had heard him preach in the marketplace or how he tenderly welcomed little children. Maybe she had witnessed his power to heal a leper or had observed his love for the poor and outcasts of society. We don't know how, but this woman had certainly had a profound encounter with the Lord of grace.

There is only one explanation for her extravagant love for Jesus: It is his extravagant love for her. "We love because he first loved us" (1 John 4:19). She had been forgiven her "many sins," and therefore, she "loved much." There is no greater manifestation of being forgiven by God than for us to love him and then others. This is the essence of what Jesus calls the "new command." "A new command I give you: Love one another. As I have loved you, so you must love one another" (John 13:34).

Jesus then says to Simon, "He who has been forgiven little, loves little." The question is not, "Who among us has more sins to be forgiven?" but "Who among us is most aware of his many sins and is astonished at the complete forgiveness we have been given in Jesus?" Simon was not less sinful than this woman; he was just far more obtuse to his real condition. Legalism does not merely make it impossible to see others as God sees them, it also keeps us from seeing ourselves as we truly are.

The woman, of course, must have observed the whole interchange between Jesus and Simon. How did she feel when she became the center of attention? Though Simon could not recognize her dignity, Jesus did. He turned to her and, with authority and tenderness, said, "Your sins are forgiven." Jesus affirmed publicly what this woman had already believed in her heart—she was completely forgiven. The same music that filled the heart of the returning prodigal son now filled hers.

Simon remained tone-deaf to this melody, but the other guests were astonished. "Who is this who even forgives sins?" To make sure that the woman had no doubt about the means of her salvation, Jesus said to her, "Your faith has saved you; go in peace."

It wasn't her tears, it wasn't her promises, it wasn't her effort. It was her faith in Jesus that brought this peace that passes all understanding.

Hard Hearts Made Malleable

When conservative religious people compare themselves with the irreligious, the liberals, and the outwardly immoral, all sense of needing God's grace disappears. That was the elder brother's problem, and Simon's problem. But when our hearts are held up to the light of the love demands of God's holy law we are devastated, we are silenced, we are speechless. We have nothing to boast in or about, for none of us loves God or man the way the law requires. Is there hope for change?

Can the elder son in me come home? Can I be found as the younger son was found? How can I return when I am lost in resentment, when I am caught in jealousy, when I am imprisoned in obedience and duty lived out as slavery? It is clear that alone, by myself, I cannot find myself. More daunting than healing myself as the younger son is healing myself as the elder son. Confronted here with the impossibility of self-redemption, I now understand Jesus' words to Nicodemus: "Do not be surprised when I say: 'You must be born from above.'" Indeed, something has to happen that I myself cannot cause to happen. I cannot be reborn from below; that is, with my own strength, with my own mind, with my own psychological insights. There is no doubt in my mind about this because I have tried so hard in the past to heal myself from my complaints and failed . . . and failed . . . and failed, until I came to the edge of complete emotional collapse and even physical exhaustion. I can only be healed from above, from where God reaches down. What is impossible for me is possible for God. "With God, everything is possible."[3]

Here is where hope begins for both returning prodigals and recovering Pharisees. We see our desperate and daily need and dive, yet again, into the ever flowing river of God's grace. It's never easy to humble ourselves, but it is always good. This need will continue until the day we are made perfect in love, when Jesus returns. The only time we will not need the gospel is when we are safely delivered to heaven.

Jump or Dive, But Get In!

My good friend John Patton once took me to a set of cliffs eighty feet above a beautiful body of water. "John, what a view! This is great, man. Why haven't you brought me here before?"

"Take off your shirt," he responded. "I didn't bring you here for the view. We're jumping in."

"What? You're crazy," I shot back. "I thought this was our picnic spot. That's a long way down and that water looks freezing."

"Scotty, the picnic is the water. Now, are you jumping or watching?"

Fear gave way to joy as I hurled myself off that cliff into the water. It was incredible. I got out and jumped again—and again and again.

How thankful I am for a friend who confronted me in love and invited me to throw myself into the river of grace. I regret that I allowed my fear and pride to keep me out of the river of God's delight for so long. That represented the first step in the process of bringing my arrogant and aloof heart to repentance and healing. The sound of music and dancing in my Father's house grows more and more distinct as I humble myself and jump again and again and again. Jump or dive, come on in!

chapter four

[NEW CREATION]

Great Expectations

The morning finds me here at heaven's door
A place I've been so many times before
Familiar thoughts and phrases start to flow
And carry me to places that I know so well
Do I fear what I don't understand
Do I not remember where I am
I stand before the great eternal throne
the one that God himself is seated on
and I have been invited to come and

Believe the unbelievable
Receive the inconceivable
See beyond my wildest imagination
Lord I come with great expectation

So wake up hope that slumbers in my soul
Stir the fire inside and make it glow
I'm trusting in a love that has no end
The Savior of the world has called me friend
And I have been invited with the Son
Oh I have been invited to come and

Believe the unbelievable
Receive the inconceivable
See beyond my wildest imagination
Lord I come with great expectation

Steven:

"Steven, put some clothes on that bare bottom of yours!" Once again my mom chased me off of my favorite chair where I would climb up to play my first guitar au naturel. I loved to hop right out of my bath and run buck naked to the kitchen and sit on one of our kitchen chairs with rattan woven seats and play away. I can remember my little eight-year-old derriere getting a checkerboard imprint as I sat there, imagining myself to be the next great guitarist to break onto the scene.

My musical dreams took on a new direction when I got my first drum set and a copy of the official *Banana Splits* TV show sound track! "One Banana, two Bananas, three Bananas, Four . . ." I sat on my drums with headphones on, music blaring, beating away until I was worn out. Music grabbed my heart and soul early.

My dad owned a music store called Chapman Music, which fed and fueled my budding passion. What a deal! I could walk into his store, take down any instrument, and give it a shot. As a junior and senior in high school, I learned to play guitar, steel guitar, bass, drums, banjo, and piano, not to mention the spoons and a mean Jew's harp! Dad, always a lover of singer-songwriters, filled the air with the music of artists like James Taylor, Glen Campbell, John Denver, and Jim Croce.

At fourteen I started teaching guitar in Dad's store. My first student later joined a band I started in college, but he went on to bigger and better things, landing a job with country star Lee Greenwood and becoming a studio sessions player.

As my love for music grew, I played in a smorgasbord of settings. Brother Herbie and I performed as the Chapman Brothers until he went off to college at the beginning of my sophomore year in high school. My musical influences expanded to include not just acoustic players like Dan Fogleberg, but also bands like the Doobie Brothers, the Atlanta Rhythm Section, the Eagles, and a host of others.

Along with being in and out of an assortment of "garage bands," I got to don one of those gaudy, hot wool uniforms as a snare drummer in the Heath High School Marching Band. I played electric guitar for the jazz ensemble and was a fill-in guitarist for a southern gospel group, for which my best friend, Denny Alvey, played bass.

The three of us who made up the rhythm section of that polyester-clad gospel quartet started our own little group called PEACE. It proved to be my first foray into the world of Christian rock. Most folk who heard our band thought of us as anything but "PEACE-ful!" We were good and loud—or was that loud and louder? Every waking moment was consumed with creating music. I couldn't get enough.

After high school, I landed a summer job with a country music extravaganza in Gatlinburg, Tennessee. It was my first out-of-town gig. The following fall, I began my studies at Georgetown College, planning on a premed major. But after one semester, I transferred to Anderson College, where I majored in music business and gave myself fully to the craft of songwriting, my first love. I came under the watchful care and mentoring of Ron Griffin and the master himself, Bill Gaither.

I seized many opportunities to play and sing during my college years. Herbie was already at Anderson, and, with another friend, we formed a group called Chapman-Henderson. The firstfruits of a career in contemporary Christian music began to emerge. If, by chance, you had visited Opryland in the summer of my college years, you probably would not have recognized the George Jones look-alike/sound-alike gracing the stage. Don't tell anybody, but that was yours truly!

While at Anderson, one of my songs, "Built to Last," was recorded by the legendary Imperials. After graduating, I married Mary Beth, and we moved to Nashville, fully expecting that I would make my mark, as well as our daily bread, as a songwriter.

But not long after we moved, I was presented with the prospect of actually recording some of the songs I had demoed for a publisher. Some folks had seen me perform in Chapman-Henderson and liked the way I "connected and communicated" my songs with the audience. This surprised me since Herbie had always been the one of us most known for his vocals. Before I knew it, I had signed my first record deal!

A few vinyl albums, CDs, hundreds of concerts, thousands of frequent flyer miles, a shelf of Dove Awards, and even a couple of Grammies later, and I found myself in the middle of my "Signs of Life" project, wondering how my own spiritual pulse is. For quite a while I had become increasingly overwhelmed by the mounting pressures and pulls associated with the success of an expanding career and ministry. "Lord, help me in the whirlwind of all of this 'stuff.' I feel like I'm losing something vital."

How did I go from being an innocent bare-bottomed eight-year-old guitarist to feeling weighed down by all the expectations placed on me? Along with new opportunities to sing and perform, I began to feel the stress of staying current with the ever-changing music scene. "Am I getting outdated? How can the next record and tour get a cool and fresh cutting edge? I'm no longer the 'new kid on the block'— do I need a makeover? Lord, what happened to the days of singing my songs and longing to see the gospel capture the hearts of whoever would listen? Why isn't this fun anymore? Where's my joy?"

Another pattern concerned me. It became easy—too easy—to use the studio to escape the mess of my world. As long as I was involved in the creative process, I could buy myself a moment of peace, the space I needed to block everything else out—at least temporarily.

Then, one year, as Easter approached, we were invited to attend a Passion play at a little Baptist church just up the road from our home. At the end of the drama, the actor who portrayed Simon Peter approached the now-empty cross of Jesus. As he gazed upon the scene of Jesus' death, the full force of his betrayal came crashing down upon Peter's soul, and he broke. Like a shaft of light piercing my conscience, the Holy Spirit gave me grace to see myself in the way Peter lived his life.

While I had been eager to jump out of my own little boat and leave my fishing nets to take the world for Jesus, a subtle shift had occurred in my soul. As much as it hurt to realize it, my music had become an obsession. I no longer controlled it. It controlled me. I stayed busy, frantic, and preoccupied.

It reminded me of when Jesus visited the home of Mary and Martha. While Mary took the time to sit at the feet of Jesus and fellowship *with* him, enjoying his presence, Martha was in the kitchen, flustered by her meal preparations *for* Jesus. My kitchen of drivenness, innocently called the "creative process," robbed me of that which matters most, a deep abiding fellowship with Jesus. I allowed too much of my identity to be bound up in doing great things *for* the Lord rather than simply enjoying being *with* him. My little kingdom of creativity was similar to Martha's kitchen, and her angry frustrated spirit mirrored mine. The creative process was becoming my drug of choice.

As Scotty and I walked through this season together, he told me something I will never forget: "Ministry can be an incredibly seductive mistress." We both reaffirmed our constant need to guard our hearts, at all costs. This proved to be the beginning of a fresh repentance, a coming back to my senses and to my first love relationship with Jesus. But as with any obsession, my ongoing need for God's grace is well-defined. As the hymn writer has well said,

> Prone to wander, Lord, I feel it,
> Prone to leave the God I love;
> Here's my heart, O take and seal it;
> Seal it for Thy courts above.

Scotty:

My Heart, Christ's Home and an Idol Factory

As a young boy I had three great loves in my life: food, fire, and fun. These three were my obsessions. Food exercised the greatest charm. I loved to eat. I never met a carbohydrate I didn't like: homemade bread, pastries, and cookies, in particular, topped the list of life's greatest joys, earning me the nickname "Meatball" by the time I was in the seventh grade. I can remember pulling out the bottom of my T-shirt like a cotton tray to empty a whole cookie jar into it. I would find a comfy place to sit and munch away like a famished hamster. At the beginning of ninth grade, I was five feet tall and weighed 170 pounds! Cute and portly, I'm told.

My first attempt to diet was a fiasco. I drank liquid diet products, assuming that it acted like calorie acid. I ate whatever I wanted, then drank a can of the stuff, fully expecting to weigh at least a pound less the next morning. If I remember correctly, I put on ten pounds in two weeks!

Then, there was my love for fire. I don't think I was a pyromaniac, but I was fascinated with making flames, stoking fires, and burning things. When I was about six, I got caught with one of my neighborhood buddies making a little fire—under his house! Both our homes got a little hot that evening as our parents lit a different kind of fire. Unfortunately, it wasn't enough to snuff out my fascination with pyrotechnics.

Instead, I broadened my interest to include fireworks. I grew up in the day of *real* firecrackers—cherry bombs and M-80s, which were equivalent to about a tenth of a stick of dynamite. I reduced the fish population in a couple of ponds by detonating a few of these waterproof beauties underwater. We used to flush them down toilets. But for the grace of God, I could be lacking fingers or eyes or both. How foolish I was!

Then I decided to learn how to smoke, though it didn't occur to me to try cigarettes. I preferred exotic smokes. I struck a match to a rolled-up paper bag for my first drag. From there I graduated to stuffing leaves into the cardboard tube inside a roll of paper towels. It barely fit into my mouth.

The third member of my trinity was fun—which is another way of saying I was allergic to work. "Just do enough to get by" was my slogan. Whatever minimized sweat and maximized pleasure was the way I chose to live. Fun, for example, was sitting in front of the TV for hours and never having read a whole book until I graduated from high school. My best friends were the Cleaver family, the Flintstones, and those delightful people of Mayberry, especially Andy and Barney. My passions were pointless and passionless. But they controlled my life.

Chief Navel Gazer

I wish the next part of the story went like this: "Then I became a Christian and everything changed. I am a new creation who wants only to please God."

If change only came that easily! Accept Jesus and your struggles will go away, your heartache will disappear, and your complexion will clear up. Unfortunately, this superficial view is not unlike what I believed for the first several years of my Christian life. Victorious Christian-living testimonies were considered true evidence of God's grace. Isn't that what the Bible teaches? Aren't we supposed to be "*more* than conquerors" as Christians?

At least, that's what you would have thought if you had heard me give my "testimony" as a young believer. But if you had spent a couple of days with me, you would have wondered who I was referring to. My understanding—or misunderstanding—of life in Christ was rooted in flawed and superficial teaching.

Martin Luther said that bad theology is the worst of all task-masters. This has been documented throughout church history. Remember when some Christians gullibly bought and believed the book entitled *Jesus Is Coming Back September 16, 1988*? Significant financial decisions were made, homes were sold, college students dropped out of school, and marriage plans were canceled—all because of a poorly written little book about the end times. When Jesus did not come back in 1988, the author simply wrote another book, stating he had miscalculated the date by one year. When Jesus did not come back in 1989, many disillusioned, embarrassed, and angry Christians had to face the consequences of their theological error.

Theological distortion damages many other things, but I am a prime example of how it corrupts *everything* else. Most of the teaching I received as a young Christian made narcissism easy for me. I believed that I was saved by grace, yes, but I also believed I could earn or forfeit God's blessing based on my performance. And being a performer, I was easily deceived by this nongospel.

Most of my early understanding of the faith, like that of many in the Jesus Movement of the '60s and '70s, came from "the school of dutiful discipleship." Filling in the blanks of all the notebooks, attending the myriad "how-to" seminars, learning the JESUS cheer, identifying the Antichrist, waiting for the Rapture—I was there!

How we loved to share our deliverance stories! I could attest that Jesus had delivered me from overeating, smoking paper bags, and hating to read. In the place of those things he gave me *new* "spiritual disciplines." It took a long time before I began to see that my new obsessions were just as self-centered and destructive as my old ones. I became obsessed with physical fitness ("taking care of the temple"), making A's in seminary (being a "student to the glory of God"), and succeeding in ministry ("bearing fruit"). In reality, all I did was replace gluttony with vanity, stupidity with sophistry, and laziness with workaholism. But these things made me feel so spiritual, as if God's grace had given me a whole new self-image.

Self-centered Grace

Looking back, and not that far back, I can see my error and that of our culture. It is nothing but self-centeredness. Once, the *London Times* asked G. K. Chesterton to respond to the question "What is the Problem in the Universe?" He answered, "I am. Sincerely, G. K. Chesterton."[1] In subtle ways, our evangelism feeds that kind of self-ism. We are led to believe that we are the point of the Christian life. How many evangelists have said something to this effect: "If no one else in the world existed, Jesus still would have died for you—that's how special you are." Sounds sweet, but what does it mean?

One of the first Christian youth musicals I participated in was called *Natural High*. The theme song said, in essence, "Don't get high on drugs, sex, or alcohol. Get high on Jesus." I don't question the integrity of the writers, but the message the listener received was: "The goal of life is personal fulfillment and satisfaction—getting high. Jesus is the right and best way to reach that high. Give him a chance."

Grace by Any Other Name . . .

In thirty years, I have learned that God's grace can be misused and abused, and there seem to be four main aberrations of this grace:

1. Greasy Grace: The Freedom Not to Take Him Seriously

Christians sometimes use grace as an excuse not to obey God. Have you ever heard someone exclaim, "Don't put me under the law; I'm under grace!" While these sentiments of the apostle Paul are appropriate in the right setting, they are seldom applied correctly. Living by grace and being obedient are not mutually exclusive. Salvation by grace and salvation by obedience *are* mutually exclusive—antithetical, in fact. But God's grace gives me a new motivation and power to obey him. We are called to the obedience of faith and love.

2. Sleazy Grace: Whoopee!

This perversion of God's grace, one of the oldest, makes grace into a carte blanche to indulge in anything one desires. There are those who have so distorted the notion of God's grace as to render it utterly meaningless. They are hedonists clothed in religious garb.

While in seminary, one of my professors told a story of a group of sixteenth-century German Christians who believed that God is most glorified and pleased when he gets to pour out grace on his children. So they reasoned and taught that the more immoral, undisciplined, irresponsible, and drunk Christians could be, the better! Since God's glory was at stake, they indulged in every vice imaginable! Paul anticipated this distortion when he wrote, "Shall we go on sinning so that grace may increase? By no means! We died to sin; how can we live in it any longer?" (Rom. 6:1–2).

3. Cheesy Grace: A Warm Fuzzy

It is dangerous to equate God's grace with a sentimentality. Grace becomes a synonym for a nice safe god who wouldn't think of sending anyone to hell. This version is proffered by those who have what I call a "Gumby-god"—one that can be shaped into any form desired.

Have you ever heard someone exclaim, "My god would never do something like that!" or "If that is what your god is like, I won't have anything to do with him. I want a god that is much different than yours." Behind these notions is the belief that we can choose the god we want, as we might choose a new car or a cup of yogurt! Get whatever pleases your taste buds.

Cheesy grace is at the heart of universalism, the belief that all humanity will be reconciled to God. The notion of eternal punishment is a sobering one, and we should never pretend it is an easy doctrine to accept. Yet to reject the clear teaching of Scripture just because it offends our sensibilities reveals more about us and our superficial understanding of grace than it does about God.

4. Measly Grace: My Hard Work Will Lead to Salvation (I Hope!)

This popular corruption reduces God's grace to his benevolent assistance in helping me earn my salvation. This version of grace is understood to be the difference between what I can do in my own strength and what I can do to "get over the hump of salvation" with a little of God's help. What arrogance is reflected in this way of thinking! There is no more prevalent perversion of grace than this.

Measly grace is expressed through the unbiblical notion that "grace is for sinners and the duties of discipleship are for the saints." In this popular heresy, it is assumed that you are either a sinner or a saint, that is, either a non-Christian or a Christian. It also assumes that the main thing a non-Christian needs is the gospel of God's grace and that the main thing a Christian needs is more instruction and exhortation in discipleship. These destructive dichotomies are not rooted in Scripture.

A Christian is a "sinner-saint," that is, someone who has been saved by God's grace and who will continue to sin until they are made perfect by God in heaven. Paul uses a startling and shocking image when he describes Christians as wicked people who have been justified by God (Rom. 4:5). We need God's grace throughout the entirety of our lives, not just at the beginning and not just in small increments along the way to get us "over the hump."

Grace-Assisted Living

Notice what these corruptions have in common. Each assumes that grace is a commodity God dispenses to make life more pleasant, more bearable. God's grace is assisted living. Each assumes that the individual is the raison d'être of God's grace. They all put man, not God, in the center, saying, "The chief end of God is to glorify man so he can enjoy himself forever."

What a contrast this is to the eighteenth-century Christians of the Westminster Assembly who proclaimed, "The chief end of man is to glorify God and enjoy Him forever." While we have been rightly busy with the question, "*What* must I do to be saved?" we have neglected to ask, "*Why* have you saved me? To what end, Father, have you lavished this grace upon me?"

Am I a New Creation?

I have worn glasses since I was eighteen. The contrast between what I see with my glasses on and with them off is scary. With my new lenses I have 20–15 vision, but without them, people look like vegetables—as though I were living in the VeggieTales.

Through the years I've come to realize my need for corrective lenses for my heart. God has been faithful to bring much-needed spiritual optometry to bear. For the first years of my Christian life, I suffered from myopia—shortsightedness. I could not see beyond my own navel!

For a long time, I read the Bible primarily, if not exclusively, in terms of myself. I saw most biblical truths through the grid of "my personal relationship with Jesus." But the Great Physician brought about healing as I learned, more often than not, that a primary conduit of his grace is other people. Two particular encounters moved me from nearsightedness to farsightedness.

While visiting a group of Christians in Nigeria, one of them said to me, "Scotty, why do you American Christians individualize everything?

You all seem to have your own little 'private Jesus.' Wasn't it Jesus who taught us to pray '*Our* Father in heaven . . .' Where is your sense of the *whole* family of God? The kingdom of God is a whole lot bigger than you realize."

I feigned sympathy at first, not wanting to seem obtuse. But the truth is, I was *blind* to what he was saying. Like good seed planted in prepared soil, his words would yield new life in due season.

Another encounter went like this: "Men and women, please turn in your Bibles to Second Corinthians 5:17."

"Awesome, we're going to study one of my favorite Scriptures," I said to myself as I sat in a classroom at Westminster Theological Seminary. I knew that verse so well. It was one of the first I memorized as a young Christian.

But as I sat in the classroom, Dr. Richard Gaffin, professor of New Testament studies, proceeded to rock my little individualistic Christian world. "Read along with me," he said. "'Therefore, if anyone is in Christ, he is a new creation; the old has gone, the new has come!' Now read from your Greek texts with me. I want you to notice a few things."

He pointed out the absence of the little clause "he is" in Greek text. "A more literal translation of this passage is: 'Therefore, if anyone is in Christ, *new creation*; the old is gone, the new has come!'" I was confused, but he continued, "I want you to understand that for Paul, the 'new creation' is not so much what the man in Christ is as an individual, but, rather, the environment, the order, the age, the world of which he has now been made a part! The old age is passing away, the new is come in Christ!"

Dr. Gaffin spoke with excitement, wanting us to see the glory of this text. He went on to explain that the apostle's frame of reference was much bigger than the individual Christian. This was Paul's way of saying, "The kingdom of God has broken in. Christians are already a part of the new order that will be fully realized when Jesus returns."

As he developed his thesis, my anger over his tampering with one of my favorite Scriptures gave way to a growing sense of peace and joy.

Before I had interpreted this verse to mean that as soon as someone accepts Jesus into their heart they are, instantaneously, a totally brand-new creature. Their old life is eradicated and newness now defines their existence.

I tried my best to live as though this were true. I claimed it and reclaimed it. After trying to keep up the illusion of having no struggles and no doubts, I decided, "Either I've misunderstood what the Bible is teaching or I'm a spiritual pigmy." But as Dr. Gaffin invited me to look at 2 Corinthians 5:17, I experienced a near Copernican Revolution in my understanding of the Christian life. The wonderful news is that God's new creation is so much bigger and more glorious than me!

Paul is not thinking about the individual Christian being a new creation as much as he is celebrating how reconciled sinners are a part of God's great plan to make *all* things new. When John wrote (John 3:16), "For God so loved the world that he gave his one and only Son, that whoever believes in him shall not perish but have eternal life," he had more than people in mind. God not only loves his people, he loves the world he made. The death of Jesus has accomplished more, dare we say it, than securing redemption for all who trust in him. Through the death of Jesus, creation itself, one day, will be redeemed!

This is not to say that the new creation will come easily. Paul says in Romans 8:22–23, "We know that the whole creation has been groaning as in the pains of childbirth right up to the present time. Not only so, but we ourselves, who have the firstfruits of the Spirit, groan inwardly as we wait eagerly for our adoption as sons, the redemption of our bodies." There will be great excitement, yes, but there will also be great struggle.

This metaphor of a mother in labor came alive as I watched my wife give birth to our first child—after twenty-five hours of labor! After a few false starts, Darlene's OB decided to induce labor. We had gone through Lamaze together and had mastered breathing and pushing—the whole routine. As the evening dragged on, Darlene said, "Honey, why don't you get something to eat? I'm not going anywhere fast." So I went across the street for a couple of hot dogs with onions.

When I returned, things started to happen pretty fast. The contractions came faster. "Sweetheart," I said, "let me help you do your breathing. Follow me." I got down in her face with my onion breath and proceeded to thoroughly disgust her. As her pain intensified, she graciously asked me to take my onion breath outside and pace with the other dads-to-be in the waiting room.

Soon, we got word that Kristin, our daughter, was in the posterior position, which meant that labor was going to be longer and more difficult for Darlene. I stayed close, in the next room, praying and weeping as I heard her pain grow more intense. The pains of her labor and the depth of her love for our daughter were great.

Later I made the connection between that event and what Paul refers to in Romans 8. Few groans can compare with those of a mother in labor. Likewise, few images match that of a mother holding a new baby, a magnificent new creation of God, in her own exhausted and caressing arms. A day is coming when the labor and travail of God's old creation, marred by sin, will give way to the glory of the new. Any dancing we do in this life is a vague shadow of the dancing we will do in that day!

So in what sense is the old gone and the new come? In the same way that Paul writes about the Christian life in Romans 8. This is, the "already and the not yet." Already the "present evil age" (2 Cor. 5:17) has been dealt a fatal blow with the first coming of Jesus, but not yet has it been eradicated. Already the "new age" (2 Cor. 5:17) has arrived with the first coming of Jesus, but it has not yet come in its fullness. We Christians live in the tension of the "already and the not yet." Nothing is either as bad as it could be nor as good as it will be. Thus, we groan inwardly and wait eagerly in patient hope for the second coming of Jesus to bring closure to the old and the fullness of the new!

I have been to Switzerland six times, and every time is as though I had never been there before. I keep going back to drink in its breathtaking beauty. It is impossible to hold the sight, sounds, and smell of the Alps in your heart for very long. You simply have to be there. In the same way, my small, unbelieving heart has to continually return to a vision of God's great plan of redemption, which will culminate in the revelation of the new heavens and the new earth. Of that glorious estate the Scripture states, "No eye has seen, no ear has heard, no mind has conceived what God has prepared for those who love him" (1 Cor. 2:9). Switzerland is but a small candle compared to the effulgent glory that will be revealed in that day.

Redeeming a Castle

So what is the big picture? All of history and everything that God has made can be seen and understood through three lenses that our Father has given us in the Scriptures: Creation, the Fall, and Redemption.

CREATION—Everything has been made by God for a purpose.
THE FALL—Everything has been corrupted and distorted by sin.
REDEMPTION—Everything is being redeemed and restored through the work of Jesus.

This threefold panorama came alive on my most recent trip to Switzerland, with Darlene and two friends. After spending a week in the Swiss Alps, we decided to branch out and take a trip to the Austrian Alps. None of us had ever been to the region of Mozart and the von Trapp Family, so we ventured forth! One friend recommended that we stay a few nights at an old castle about three hours southwest of Salzburg in the little village of Mittersill.

So we made our way to Schloss (Castle) Mittersill. Slaphappy and weary from our extended trip, we were grateful when our gracious host drove us through the massive gates into the castle courtyard. It was late at night, and a heavy downpour kept us from seeing much. Our new friend, Ruddy, walked us up a long, winding staircase to our rooms on the third level. Like an actor in an old King Arthur movie, I kept waiting for an armor-clad knight to appear from around the corner, brandishing a torch and a sword. It was eerie! But being exhausted, we collapsed in our beds and fell quickly into a deep slumber.

The next morning we awoke to our first day of castle life and were given the history of this remarkable place. Originally built in 1190 at the base of the Austrian Alps, the castle enjoyed four centuries of life before being destroyed in a peasants' revolt in 1560. After being rebuilt, it had served some rather dark purposes during the Counter-Reformation, when witches were tried in the chapel and lowered into a cauldron of boiling water through the floor—unless they recanted.

During the German invasion of Austria, the Nazis captured the castle, and more chapters of evil history were written as they used it to spread the regime of the Third Reich. After the war, a group of wealthy Austrians bought the castle and turned it into a successful hunt club. On the ground floor, in a room full of castle memorabilia, hang pictures of some notable Americans who visited the club in its heyday as a retreat for the rich and famous. We saw photographs of Clark Gable, Gina Lolabrigeda, Bing Crosby, and Bob Hope, among others.

After another fire destroyed much of the castle, it sat vacant for several years until a group of Christians bought it at auction. It was then "redeemed" as a training center for InterVarsity Christian Fellowship, an international ministry to college students. After several years, Schloss Mittersill was converted to an independent Christian Study Center and school of discipleship, welcoming men and women from around the world to study the Word of God. It has also become a strategic place for training new Christian leaders from eastern Europe to spread the gospel in the regions now hungry for the Good News of Jesus.

The story of this castle is a grand example of what God is doing throughout his world. This is the big picture of redemption! Like Schloss Mittersill, God created his world with a wonderful design and purpose. Through the Fall, sin and death have spread, wreaking havoc and evil everywhere. But God has purchased back—redeemed—his world through his Son, Jesus, and is actively restoring all things to reflect his glory. This process is under way right now, and it will be brought to completion when Jesus comes back at the end of history. Redemption has been accomplished and is being wondrously applied!

The Kingdom of God—The Reign of Grace

This glorious promise of the new creation is what Jesus called "the kingdom of God." Jesus made reference to the kingdom over a hundred times in the four Gospels, while he only mentioned the church twice. Through metaphor, simile, imagery, allegory—our Lord continually spoke to his disciples and preached to the crowds about the "already and the not yet" of God's kingdom. He warned of its judgment and he gloried in its promises.

With the arrival of the Messiah, the kingdom has come in a dramatic way. Old Testament prophecies of a "Wonderful Counselor, Mighty God, Everlasting Father, and Prince of Peace" have begun to be fulfilled in him. His "government and peace," which take root in the hearts of individuals, will one day spread to every nation of the world and every sphere of created life. Of our blessed King, Abraham Kuyper, prime minister of the Netherlands, once proclaimed, "There is not one inch in the entire area of our human life about which Christ, who is sovereign of all, does not cry out, 'Mine!'"[2] The mustard seed of grace will become a massive tree of life.

As I read the following words from Isaiah, I am left breathless and speechless:

> The wolf will live with the lamb, the leopard will lie down with the goat, the calf and the lion and the yearling together; and a little child will lead them. The cow will feed with the bear, their young will lie down together, and the lion will eat straw like the ox. The infant will play near the hole of the cobra, and the young child put his hand into the viper's nest. They will neither harm nor destroy on all my holy mountain, for the earth will be full of the knowledge of the Lord as the waters cover the sea. (11:6–9)

This glorious kingdom can best be thought of as God's sovereign reign over his people (and over all things) wherever he places them throughout history—from the Garden of Eden to the "new heaven and the new earth." It is a reign of grace that will come in its fullness only when Jesus returns to bring history to a conclusion and establish God's eternal kingdom of righteousness, peace, and joy.

A series of painful eureka moments have made me realize how kingdomless my understanding of the Christian life has been. To take the grace of God out of the context of his kingdom is like taking the song out of Pavarotti, the Alps out of Switzerland, the dance out of Fred Astaire, basketball from Michael Jordan, and baseball from Mark McGwire. Don't do it! It's not meant to be. The kingdom does not exist apart from God's grace, and the grace of God cannot be understood accurately apart from the kingdom.

Jesus told many parables describing the nature of the kingdom. "The kingdom of heaven is like treasure hidden in a field. When a man found it, he hid it again, and then in his joy went and sold all he had and bought that field. Again, the kingdom of heaven is like a merchant looking for fine pearls. When he found one of great value, he went away and sold everything he had and bought it" (Matt. 13:44–46).

The kingdom calls for a whole new set of values and treasures. The joy of "owning" the kingdom is greater than the joy of holding on to everything else. There is only one treasure worth selling everything to have. The transcendent value of the kingdom of God's grace is equaled by its transforming power. This pearl of great value is like a Trojan horse of God's love. It comes into our lives not to be possessed but to possess, to infiltrate every sphere of our lives and to liberate us not to love our lives so much as to shrink from death (Rev. 12:11)— to consider our lives worth nothing, if only we may finish the race and complete the task the Lord Jesus has given us—the task of testifying to the gospel of God's grace (Acts 20:24).

We will either be obsessed with smoking paper bags, making A's in seminary, making a lot of money, wearing a size-6 dress, building successful ministries, getting a record deal, retiring at age forty-five, getting on the mission field, having sex, having the perfect little Christian family—in short, we will either be obsessed with ourselves or with the only magnificent obsession, the kingdom of God.

part two

[CLUELESS MEN IN NEED OF GRACE]

How do we learn about our great need for God's grace? What moves us from self-centeredness toward God's transforming love? Perhaps God's most potent and effective means is relationships. In other people we discover the pervasiveness of our selfishness. In those relationships we see, taste, and receive the grace that sets our hearts free.

A friend once told me, "The Christian life wouldn't be so bad if it weren't for people!" Family and friends can be both our bane and our boon, both our woe and our weal, our idols and a means of grace, all at the same time. The following chapters give us a chance to share stories of the different relationships that God has used, and continues to use, to bring disruption and redemption to our hearts.

chapter five

[FOOLISHNESS, FIG LEAVES, AND THE FATHER'S LOVE]

I Will Be Here

Tomorrow morning if you wake up
And the sun does not appear
I, I will be here
If in the dark we lose sight of love
Hold my hand and have no fear
'Cause I, I will be here

I will be here when you feel like being quiet
When you need to speak your mind, I will listen
And I will be here when the laughter turns to crying
Through the winning, losing and trying, we'll be together
'Cause I will be here

Tomorrow morning if you wake up
And the future is unclear
I, I will be here
As sure as the seasons were made for change
Our lifetimes were made for these years
So I, I will be here

I will be here, so you can cry on my shoulder
When the mirror tells us we're older, I will hold you
And I will be here to watch you grow in beauty
And tell you all the things you mean to me
I will be here

I will be true to the promise I have made
   To you and to the one who gave you to me
    I will be here
     And just as sure as the seasons were made for change
     Our lifetimes were made for these years
     So I, I will be here
    We'll be together
   'Cause I will be here

Steven:

Gettin' Fired Up for Marriage

"Lord, light a fire under me! I don't want to be an average husband!" I prayed that prayer with utter sincerity just a few months after hanging up my wedding tuxedo. It didn't take Mary Beth and me long to realize that marriage would be a prime opportunity for us to either grow in grace or to resort to "Christian cannibalism"—"biting and devouring one another" as believers in Galatia were apparently prone to do (Gal. 5:15). We both wanted God to teach us how to love one another well. Within a year he began to answer that prayer.

Simply put, Mary Beth was pregnant—after only seven months of holy headlock—I mean, wedlock. To say that we were shocked is an understatement. Mary Beth quit her job, and our one-bedroom apartment in Antioch, Tennessee, needed either to grow a nursery or we would have to move to one with two bedrooms. Guess which happened?

After a few months in our new apartment, little Emily had arrived. No sooner had we begun to settle in than an exciting new opportunity presented itself. A good friend let us know about some affordable houses that were being built in Lavergn, a little town not far from where we lived. The prospect of having a house payment that was not much more than what we were paying for rent excited us.

The doorbell rang. "You guys ready to go house hunting?" Our realtor got us so excited about the idea of having our own little nest for five-week-old Emily.

Now, I should explain that we usually entered and exited our apartment through the back door, which gave us a chance to check everything on our way out and to load the car with all of the paraphernalia you need for a newborn. But this time, the three of us just bolted out the front door in the joyful anticipation of buying our first house.

After the excitement of looking at houses and dreaming about "what if," our realtor drove us home. We had only been gone about an hour, and as we approached our apartment we noticed a lot of commotion—and then the ominous sight of fire trucks. Our racing hearts became racing feet as it became obvious that our apartment was the object of tons of high-pressure water. I took off running and Mary Beth followed, leaving Emily in the car seat. Our realtor had the presence of mind to pick her up, while our spirits were nose-diving. How could this be?

Our landlord walked up as we were just beginning to assess the damage. "According to the firemen, the fire started in the kitchen. Something apparently was left on." Indeed, Mary Beth left the baby bottle sterilizer on and since we left through the front door we simply forgot to check everything on our way out. Could the pain be any more intense? The structure remained intact, but the water and smoke damage was pervasive.

I poked around through the cabinets and found broken shards of wedding china—which had never been used. As hard as it was, it was a good reminder that, like all of our so-called treasures, even these precious gifts from friends will one day end up as ashes. Still, as a young husband and father, I found myself ill prepared for this trial. Quoting a few Scriptures, tugging on my bootstraps, rolling up my sleeves—all of it was to no avail.

The first glimmer of grace came through our good friends, Tony and Cindy Ellenberg. They welcomed us into their home and into their hearts. Tony promised me, "Steven, you'll get through this. A time will come when you'll be able to look back with peace. I know it's true because my mom has burned up three different kitchens in her life! Trust me, you'll laugh one day." Tony's words brought encouragement, but circumstances would get a whole lot worse before they would get much better.

Tensions mounted on many fronts. I felt trapped in the middle of so many conflicting opinions about what was best for the young Chapman newlyweds with child. Never had I been more vulnerable. The date April 13, 1986, will stand out in my memory forever. We were dirt-poor and continued to sleep on the Ellenbergs' floor with

Emily in a crib. Within forty-eight hours, Uncle Sam would claim the last of our meager savings to finance the federal government for another year.

I reached my limit and hit my knees in despair. Job had cried, "Though he slay me, yet will I bless him." My cry sounded more like: "God, where are you? Why won't you show up? I've always tried to give you credit for everything, so why don't you get involved? Where else can I go but to you?" God welcomed my anguish and loved me as his troubled son. For one of the first times in my life, I experienced true brokenness. While I had been busy seeing to everyone else's need for grace, I had been clueless about my own.

Through this experience, I chose to move toward Mary Beth rather than pull away from her into my usual self-sufficiency and private pity party. This represented the beginning of genuine intimacy in our marriage, a wonderful taste of what could be. Before long we were able to buy one of those cute little houses in Lavergn. Could it be that my long term in the school of husband-grace was about to culminate in graduation? No chance!

One day, shortly after moving into our new home, I went by the Ellenbergs to pick up our mail. I noticed a letter from a fire-insurance company. I thought, *That's odd. We didn't have any renters' insurance on our belongings. I wonder what they want.* Upon opening the letter, I realized that the company wasn't trying to sell us a policy—they were collecting on an old fire: "Dear Mr. Chapman. Because of negligence on your part you owe us $13,000 for damage from the aforementioned fire." How could this be? Mary Beth and I went from the penthouse of joy to the outhouse of heartache in the time it took to read one business letter. "Honey, what can we sell? What can we do?"

But a gift of grace soon arrived in the form of a Christian lawyer named David Maddox. He wrote a letter on our behalf humbly pleading our case. The insurance company responded by reducing the liability to $8,000. Since that number could just as well have been $80,000 in terms of our financial world, David once again appealed to them for mercy. The insurance company then reduced our debt to

$2,000, payable in $50 monthly increments. We were overjoyed! The day we sent the last payment to the insurance company we got on our knees and gave God thanks for freedom!

To love a wife the way Christ has loved the church requires more humility than resides in the soul of the average man. God began a work in the first two years of my marriage that continues today. I have always considered it God's wisdom and sense of humor that just before the fire ravaged our apartment I wrote one of my most requested songs, "Hiding Place." It refers, of course, to Corrie ten Boom's famous book in which she describes her struggle to experience the grace of God amidst deeply trying circumstances. In that time of my life, her struggle became my struggle. I am no less in need of God's grace today than I was after the fire. The good news is that I am no longer surprised by my need.

These are the words that helped carry me through those years of trial:

Hiding Place

in the distance I can see the storm clouds
coming my way
and I need to find a shelter
before it starts to rain [or burn!]

so I turn and run to You Lord
you're the only place to go
where unfailing love surrounds me
when I need it most

You're my hiding place
safe in Your embrace
I'm protected from the storm that rages
when the waters rise
and I run to hide
Lord, in You I find my hiding place

I'm not asking You to take away
my troubles Lord

'cause it's through the stormy weather
I learn to trust You more

so I thank You for Your promise
I have come to know
Your unfailing love surrounds me
when I need it most

so let Your people seek You
while You may be found
'cause You're our only refuge
when the rain comes pouring down

Scotty:

Scotty . . . Where Are You?

It was either on the second or the third date (the debate still goes on!) that I asked Darlene to marry me. Fearing rejection, I didn't even let her respond immediately: "Sweetheart, I have something to ask you, but don't answer until you've prayed for a week or two. Will you marry me?" That sounds mature, but since I feared she would say no, I thought I could at least have a week or two, dreaming of what it would be like to be married to the most beautiful girl I had ever met.

Darlene and I had met in a little house church near Burlington, North Carolina, about a week after she had become a Christian. She literally glowed with the beauty of spiritual rebirth and an awesome tan! The first night I saw her I thought, "That's the woman I want to marry."

At the end of the Bible study I told the couple in whose home we were meeting, "I think I've met my wife. Is this testosterone or the testimony of God's Spirit—or both?" They agreed to pray for the Lord's wisdom.

Through friends, I got Darlene's address and started writing her. In the first letter from her that graced my mailbox, I found out, to my delight, that she wasn't dating anyone at the time. During the next eighteen months we built a friendship through sharing Scripture, prayer requests, going to Bible studies, and encouraging each other in the Lord.

Eventually, when she said yes and we got engaged, I felt as though I had won the Publisher's Clearinghouse Sweepstakes. I was ecstatic. It was too good to be true. I remember thinking that it would be just my luck for Jesus to come back before she said, "I do." The fact that I wanted to be married to her more than I wanted to be in heaven says a lot more about how little my life was shaped by the gospel than it speaks of the depth of my love for Darlene.

On May 5, 1972, we began our life together. I doubt that anyone has entered marriage more ill prepared than I was, and ever since that first day of our honeymoon right up to today, twenty-six years later, I have heard the voice of my heavenly Father persistently ask the same question he posed to the original foolish husband in the Garden of Eden, "Where are you?" (Gen. 3:9).

The Grace of Pursuit

It is a gift to be pursued by God! I only came to understand that after much hiding behind many fig leaves. When God asked his first son, Adam, his whereabouts, it wasn't as though God couldn't see through the trees, bushes, and rocks. The Father wasn't asking for his own benefit, but for Adam's. For, you see, it was *Adam* who had lost his bearings. He had eaten the forbidden fruit, and as a result, he was the prototype of the clueless husband, the first prodigal. But though he may have left home, he couldn't leave the Father's heart.

What a penetrating question that is: "Where are you?" For Adam, the answer could only be given in relation to where he had been before eating the fruit. Few Scriptures are more astonishing and inviting than the description of life in the Garden of Eden before the Fall. Genesis 2:25 says, "The man and his wife were both naked, and they felt no shame."

These thirteen words describe life the way our Father designed it: God's people, living in perfect relationship and harmony with each other and with everything in creation—before his face. *This* is the first description of the kingdom of God! What an image—"naked and unashamed." They were naked physically, emotionally, spiritually, intellectually. Can you imagine what it would be like to feel no shame, to feel no brokenness, to have no reason *not* to make eye contact with anyone—including God?

But after the Fall, Adam and Eve tried to cover their newfound shame with fig leaves. So God asked, "Where are you?" The peaceful voice of the One with whom they walked in manifest joy in the cool of the day now elicits fear and hiding. An opportunity to confess their sin and humble themselves before God is lost. Instead of receiving grace, they extend blame—they blame God, Satan, and each other. "It's the woman *You* gave me. . . . It's the serpent."

Nevertheless, to this proud man and woman, God promised redemption and provided a covering with which fig leaves cannot compare (Gen. 3:15, 21). That promise found its fulfillment in the gift of God's Son, Jesus, who clothes us with the robe of his righteousness and beautifies us with garments of grace. There is no other effective way to deal with our sin and its shame.

One Month and Counting

"Scotty, where are you?" I heard God ask that question on the evening of Darlene's and my first-month anniversary. To celebrate the completion of four weeks of marital bliss, I took Darlene to one of the finest restaurants in town. We sat at a great table with fresh-cut flowers as violin players strolled by—romance was in the air. Our waiter promptly arrived and ran through the specialties. I remember saying, "Honey, order anything you want."

I don't recall what entrée she ordered, but when she said, "And I'd like butter and sour cream on my baked potato," I immediately shot back with a tone and body language that conveyed volumes—"Butter *and* sour cream?" You see, I was the calorie control clerk in our marriage—after all, wasn't a good Christian wife supposed to submit to her husband in *all* things?

I will never forget the look in her eyes as they began to fill with tears. The violin players quickly arrived, assuming their music had deeply touched these young lovers. I backpedaled as fast as I could and started grabbing for every fig leaf in sight, but Darlene had already gotten the message. She tasted my foolishness, and it couldn't be sent back to the kitchen. She understood my meaning—that her physical beauty meant a lot to me, and as a former "meatball," I wasn't going to let either of us lose our youthful shapes. I can still feel the sadness and pain of that evening.

At that point, I heard the voice beckon, "Scotty, where are you?" Still, I was too proud to move toward brokenness and confession.

Then, one night, a couple years later, Darlene sat straight up in bed and blurted out in deep pain, "I don't have any idea who you are."

That's the most absurd thing I've ever heard, I thought, as I shook myself awake. We had been married for almost three years—of course, she knew me. I proceeded to rattle off a whole list of things that she knew about me, enough facts and data to fill pages of job applications.

Looking back, I can see that Darlene's cry was similar to that of the father's in *Fiddler on the Roof,* when one day he asks his wife, "Do you love me?"

"Do I what?" she responds with irritation.

"Do you *love* me?" he repeats.

She answered this way: "For all these years I have cooked your meals, made your bed, raised your children. . . . What do you mean do I love you?" I think her husband longed for a different response.

I know Darlene did. But being married to me for three years had made her feel unnecessary, alone.

Again, I heard the voice. "Scotty, where are you?" I started to pay a little more attention.

A Fish Named "Hogan House"

Then God sent one of his larger fish to swallow me—à la Jonah. I sat in a room full of boxes, most taped shut. The egglike smell of fresh paint filled the house as intensely as the emotions that pressed me deeper into the sofa. Darlene, eight months pregnant with our second child, carried an even heavier heart—and rightfully so. Welcome to Nashville!

The move from Winston-Salem proved to be more difficult than I could have dreamed. Believe it or not, I had bought our new house without my wife ever having seen it! It seemed like a great purchase at the time. I had been called to be the new youth pastor of a large church, but with my small salary, I couldn't find the same housing quality in Nashville as I had in Winston-Salem. After one failed search together, Darlene entrusted me with the high calling of securing the "right little place" for our young and expanding family. Being pregnant, she was unable to travel.

Like the shock you feel when you compare the picture in the catalog to what actually arrives in the mail, my phone-call description of the "Hogan House" (so named because it was on Hogan Avenue) did not represent the reality Darlene experienced that painful August afternoon. She had arrived in Nashville, and upon seeing the house for the first time, she asked, "Honey, where's the backyard?" Like any mom worth her weight in Winnie-the-Pooh wallpaper, she cared about safe, quality play space for our three-year-old daughter, Kristin, and son-to-be, Scott.

Two weeks before, when she had asked me whether the house had a backyard, I had told her, "Sweetheart, you'll love the setting. There's a swing set, a creek, and it has almost an acre of trees and grass. It's in a nice quiet neighborhood, close to the church and good shopping." I had left out one minor detail, however. The house sat on the back edge of the property line, leaving only a driveway separating it from our neighbor's house. We're talkin' zero backyard! *Surely our kids'll enjoy a big front yard as much as a backyard,* I reasoned to myself as the ink dried on the real-estate contract.

As I walked Darlene around to the front yard, I fully expected her to say, "Wow, what a great place for our kids, honey!" Instead, we stumbled upon a young couple next to our creek—making out! Hello family values! Cars began whizzing by, making this corner lot seem more like a banked turn at the Daytona 500 than a quaint residential community. If looks could kill! If tears could drown! Has silence ever been more deadly? Darlene felt so betrayed, so uncared for. I wanted to disappear. I've never felt a greater sense of failing someone I love.

The fiasco immobilized me. What a situation! Forty-eight hours after Darlene had arrived from Winston-Salem—where she had left friends and trusted doctors—there I sat, spiritually and emotionally naked—and very ashamed. Scotty Smith, the new youth pastor, called to resurrect the fledgling youth program in a major Nashville church, a young man of faith and power! What a joke! Little did I realize the enormous importance of this despairing moment. God was humbling a proud man. "Scotty," the voice now sounded more like a shout, "Where are you?"

A Chain Saw of Grace

After we had been married ten years, with two kids and with many hurts behind us, I sensed the need to be better equipped to care for the growing number of people coming to me for counsel. So three of my friends and I went to a piece of frozen wasteland called Winona Lake, Indiana, where, at Grace Seminary, Dan Allender and Larry Crabb had built a discipling and teaching ministry in the early '80s. As I drove into this little conservative community, I remember thinking, "This place is so cold, white, flat, and ugly"—which was actually an appropriate metaphor for the condition of my heart.

I went to Winona Lake hoping that Dan, my friend and former seminary classmate, would give me some tools to help me face my increasingly complex counseling situations in Nashville. In reality, God's plan was not to equip me but to dismantle me. Have you ever had someone open you up with a chain saw? I felt as though Dan laid me out on a big marble slab and proceeded to perform an autopsy on my dead heart. It was a week of experiencing the relentless mercy of our Father and the hope of resurrection. God aims to free us, not to shame us.

It came about this way. One day, after listening to me ramble on about my childhood, family, and marriage, Dan sat up in his chair and asked one of the most important questions anyone has ever asked. "Scotty, why is there such a lack of quiet in your soul? Your many words concern me." In the language of Eden, his words meant, "Scotty, where are you?"

I had just told Dan about my forty years of painful experiences as though I were reading from an encyclopedia. Without a smile, he asked, "And where's your passion, the tears, the longings?" I'm usually quick on my feet, but when Dan asked that, my knees buckled. I was speechless. I couldn't look him in the eye because he had become the laser sharp conduit of God's voice and Spirit.

Over the next couple days Dan invited me to face other issues. My shyness, for instance, he identified as shame and contempt, for which I needed healing and repentance. What I considered faith and confidence in God's sovereignty, Dan helped me see as a fat layer of self-protection, keeping me from really knowing and worshiping God. Dan challenged me to ponder why I love so poorly, why I'm afraid of intimacy, why my knowledge of God is based on theory instead of experience. In doing all this, he became the means by which "grace" was transformed into more than just a Bible word to me. A window opened to my soul.

Dan gave me the gift of understanding the relationship between my past wounds and my present sins. To understand our deepest hurts can help us recognize the foolish ways of our own hearts.

The Birth of Self-protection Through Death

Of the events I shared with Dan, one stood out. He red flagged it for our deeper consideration. When I was eleven, my mother was killed in an automobile accident. She had been the center of my universe, and suddenly, she was gone. No good-bye—nothing. Death came to me too early with its full force and fury.

In response, I made the curious decision not to believe the obvious. I refused to go to the funeral home to see her body. With defiance, I determined not to even look at her casket during the funeral. I simply denied she was gone. Mom's death, understandably, devastated my dad. She filled his world with beauty and tenderness, two things he lacked as a child. While my older brother, and only sibling, handled this tragedy better than any of us, still, we all failed to connect as a family after this tragedy. Not once did the three of us sit down and share what we had just gone through. We never talked, never touched, never wept. We just did the best we could, retreating to whatever anesthetic would dull our pain. We were three lonely members of the same family, left to make sense of the merciless catastrophe of having a loved one ripped from our embrace.

As an eleven-year-old, I was the least equipped to deal with the loss. I wasn't a Christian, though I am not sure that would have made a difference to me at the time. Thirty-eight-year-old moms aren't supposed to die. I vacillated between crying for and wanting to "get over it." I learned to despise my tears. I made an unconscious commitment never to be hurt like that again, at any price. That commitment became an inviolate law when, after dating the same girl throughout high school, she too died in a car wreck while we were freshmen in college.

Early in my Christian life I learned to "spiritualize" away any pain, to put a big Romans 8:28 Band-Aid on my broken heart. I spent a lot of energy trying to convince others, and myself, that everything was okay because "God was bringing good things out of hard things." Looking back, I can see how fast I had to run to keep from dealing with my deep, deep hurts.

That's where Dan's love made a difference. While he rightfully identified my losses as never having been appropriately grieved, he forced me to look at the ugly, dead way I had responded. "Do you see how you have robbed the people you say you love by never lingering at your mom's grave? God's love is courageous; it's bold, but you're living like a coward." His words rang true—and they hurt. But he refused to let me be a victim or make excuses for loving poorly. In my commitment never to hurt again, I basically chose to worship an idol—self-protection.

When I got married, the deadly cancer rooted in my heart said, "Darlene, I'm going to love you, but not so much that I will go into agony if you were to die." This evil affected all my relationships, not simply as a husband, but also as a father, friend, and pastor. You can see why Darlene felt she lived with a stranger.

Dan gave me one parting gift, though it actually enraged me at first. Being full of fresh insight, I asked him, "Tell me what to do in my marriage. How can I love Darlene better?"

He knew I was asking for a checklist, something manageable, a means by which I could make him proud of me. Legalism dies hard. Laughing derisively in a way that said, "Scotty, you're better than that," he simply said, "Scotty, for the first time just go and be an honest man in her life."

It has been fifteen years since that week in cold, white, flat, ugly Winona Lake. God has been faithful. The only thing I boast in is the knowledge that there has been sufficient grace for the ensuing journey. Since that time with Dan, Darlene and I have had some of the most remarkable times of intimacy that I could have ever dreamed of. There have also been times when it seemed that God was asking too much of us. The "already and not yet" of the new creation, as we continually learn, is a part of Christian marriage as well!

From time to time, God still asks, "Scotty, where are you?" But that voice never brings fear now, only more grace and a willingness to grow. I don't bow to the god of self-protection as often as I used to, but when I do, it takes less time to recognize what's going on in my heart. My tears just embarrass me now, I no longer despise them. It is so much easier to run home to Jesus.

[MODELS AND MENTORS: THOSE WHO SHAPE US]

The Walk

I've got a Grandpa Rudd
He gave thirty years to the lumberyard
Loving his family and working hard
Got a faith like a solid rock
He's just doing the walk

I've got a friend named Larry
He sends me letters from a foreign land
He moved there with his kids and his pretty wife
Mary
To answer a holy call
He's just doing the walk

You can run with the big dogs
You can fly with the eagles
You can jump through all the hoops
And climb the ladder to the top
But when it all comes down
You know it all comes down to the walk

There's a man I know
He said He'd come to show us the way
He died on a cross and He rose from the grave
and proved He was more than talk
He taught us the walk

And now I'm singing my songs
Standing up on a big, bright stage
And I do my dance while the music plays
but when the music stops
Am I doing the walk

You can run with the big dogs
You can fly with the eagles
You can jump through all the hoops
And climb the ladder to the top
But when it all comes down
You know it all comes down to this
Do justly, love mercy
Walk humbly with your God

'Cause you can run with the big dogs
You can fly with the eagles
You can jump through all the hoops
And climb the ladder to the top
but when it all comes down
You know it all comes down, down, down, down, down
To the walk

Steven:

"Mentoring" is trendy. Whether for sports, business, or the arts, you can find discussion groups, literature, and websites on the importance of having a mentor. As Christians, we should welcome this, for walking humbly as a student of someone more mature is deeply rooted in the Scriptures. Mentors often move us from simply *talking* about grace to being transformed by it.

Mentor relationships are everywhere in the Bible: Moses and Joshua, Elijah and Elisha, Naomi and Ruth, Paul and Barnabas—the list goes on. But the epitome of all mentoring relationships is the one Jesus shared with the ordinary men he called disciples. The Gospels record how our Lord poured his life into these twelve unlikely individuals and how they became the sturdy foundation upon which Jesus built his church.

To study Jesus' three-year relationship with his protégés is to learn that the best mentoring doesn't primarily take place in a classroom but in the laboratory of life—whether in a storm-tossed boat, a field of corn, the Judean wilderness, or in a huge crowd. It's often messy and not always successful. There's nothing cool about it. To have a mentor is not a symbol of prestige, like having a new guitar, sports car, or piece of stereo equipment. It's a tutelage of the soul—it's seeing what a mess you are and how desperate you are for God's grace. Are you sure you want this kind of mentoring?

The truth is that everyone already has mentoring relationships. We all have coaches and unofficial mentors. Our lives are being shaped, by design or default, by those to whom we have given access and power over our minds and hearts. But our goal should be to be increasingly more intentional about those to whom we surrender such influence. "He who walks with the wise grows wise, but a companion of fools suffers harm" (Prov. 13:20).

Treasure in Jars of Clay

Reflecting on our mentors stirs up all kinds of feelings. It can be both humbling and a cause for joy. It's easy, too easy to take people for granted. It might seem ironic that I would put my mom and dad at the top of my list of mentors in the faith. I've already shared the story of their divorce, but that in no way negates the profound spiritual influence they had on my life.

My mom loved the Bible and convinced me of its trustworthiness. I still have a vivid image of her sending me out to the school bus with her favorite verse: "Trust in the LORD with all of your heart and lean not [whoosh!—the yellow bus doors close] on your own under-standing; in all your ways acknowledge him and . . ." Her voice would trail off, but her presence would stay with me throughout the day. She wanted to see her baby get established in the Word of God.

Dad gave me the gift of prayer and repentance, and he modeled both. I have one rich childhood memory of being in our front yard as Dad, Herbie, and I pulled up a tree with a four-wheel-drive Jeep. My dad wanted to put in a garden, and the tree was in the way. We weren't exactly trained arbor-culturalists so the tree took quite a beating. Dad felt so guilty about damaging this innocent bit of God's creation that he had us dig another hole to replant the tree. His tender heart had a deep impact on me. "Herbie, Steven, I want you to hold hands with me and your mom around this tree and let's pray that God will forgive us and cause this tree to grow big and strong." A part of me felt silly as cars passed us, holding hands around a little tree, but another part was pro-foundly moved by my dad's repentant, prayerful heart. That little sapling is now a massive shade tree giving comfort and beauty to the neighborhood and a reminder to me of God's faithfulness.

A Burning Heart for God

Brother Al Henson, senior pastor of the Lighthouse Baptist Church, gave me one of my first glimpses of a man "on fire for God." Al was our faithful pastor when we first moved to the Nashville area, and he, in particular, loved us through the trial of having all of our belongings destroyed when our apartment burned. Consistently, he "burned" every Saturday evening at the front of our sanctuary, on his knees and sometimes on his face, as he pleaded with God for the services the next day. Whether there was someone with him or not, it made no difference. He showed me what being comfortably alone with God looks like, what it means to follow Jesus in aloneness.

As newlyweds, Mary Beth and I came under his wise counsel and passionate heart. He walked and prayed with us in those stretching stages of young adulthood, helping lay a solid foundation in our marriage, family, and in my ministry. "Steven," he used to say over and over, "light obeyed increases the light, and darkness pursued increases the darkness." Brother Al introduced me to the "Himalayas of the knowledge of God," helping me understand that the more I learn of God and his ways the more I will realize how little I know.

Grace Is So Much More than a Word

I have had the privilege of meeting some extraordinary Christian leaders, but none has made a greater impression than Chuck Colson. God brought us together, and it has been my honor to invest time and heart in the work of Prison Fellowship. Chuck has enabled me to take my music into many prison facilities during the course of my concert tours—but that's the easiest thing he has done for me.

My first encounter with Chuck came through his book *Loving God*. I can still remember being riveted to each page as I read about his experiences of going behind prison walls and sharing the grace of God through cell bars with those awaiting their fate on death row. As I read, I thought, "God, how do you work in a man's heart to give him that kind of bold love? If only I could walk alongside such a man of faith in a death-row cell block someday, but that will never happen." Oh me of little faith!

Later, as I worked on ideas for my album *Heaven in the Real World*, I came across some quotes by Chuck that gave me an idea for a couple of songs. I longed for an opportunity to speak with him directly and get some of his input on the themes I felt compelled to write about.

Then one day the phone rang. My heart skipped a beat, because a phone conversation had been arranged between Chuck's office and mine, and I suspected that this was his call coming in.

"Hello, Steven. This is Chuck Colson calling."

"Hello, Mr. Colson. Thank you so much for taking the time to talk with me. This is a real honor for me."

"Please, Steven, call me Chuck."

Thus began a wonderful friendship—and Chuck's mentoring continues to shape the way I think about life and ministry. And to think that I had been afraid to even hope for such an opportunity. God truly does give good gifts.

It was a bright sunny day as I emptied my pockets before passing through the metal detectors. No, I was not boarding a plane for yet another concert date. I stood at the entrance to the Michigan City Correctional Institute, a maximum security prison in Northern Indiana. I felt both excited and nervous as I anticipated visiting death row for the first time. Every preconceived image of life within prison I had obtained from film, news clips, and a child's imagination ran through my mind.

"Steven!" I heard the ring of that familiar voice from across the room.

"Hi, Chuck, how are you?" It still felt kind of strange calling this hero of the faith of mine by his first name, but it also felt reassuring to know I was with a friend. He explained that prior to our worship service on the prison yard, we would be visiting inmates on death row, including one man who had become a Christian forty years earlier. The ministry of Prison Fellowship had become a primary means of discipleship and nurture for him, even as Chuck had become one of his best friends.

I stayed close to my new buddy and mentor as he navigated our way through the series of iron-gated entries. Each set of doors would electronically open and then close behind us before the next set would do the same. What an eerie feeling. Eventually we began our journey down the long hallway lined with cells inhabited by sons, fathers, and grandfathers who were paying the price for some terrible crime committed.

I watched my teacher intently as he offered grace to those we encountered. Whether it was simply a smile, a word, a handshake through the bars and many times a prayer, Chuck was showing me what it means to treat all men with dignity and respect. I'm not sure I have ever met anyone who can so freely love in the most difficult of situations a segment of society that appears to be so unlovable.

I tried to emulate him as I grew a little more confident. I listened to the sad lament of a grandfather who showed me the pictures of his grandchildren whom he had wounded deeply with his tragic choices. Together, Chuck and I prayed with one African-American brother who greeted us with a smile and a joy that could only be traced to the life-giving grace of God. He, like many others, spoke with great remorse and sorrow for the lives of those affected most by the evil they had done, namely, the victims and their loved ones. This brother went on to tell us how God had given him life and freedom even though he was deserving of death. He told us how he had been and would continue to be praying for us as we carried the gospel to others inside of prison, as well as those outside the stone walls. In some ways he seemed to be a whole lot more free in his prison cell than many of us who will never see the inside of such a prison.

Our cell block walk culminated with a visit to Chuck's friend Bob (not his real name) inside a heavily secured room. I would describe it as the equivalent of a large iron-caged room inside two other iron cages. Bob was a large man, and when he shuffled into the room in shackles and handcuffs I felt a surge of fear come over me. However, as we all talked, I only saw the evidence of a man who had been changed from death to life. I watched as Chuck and Bob embraced for the first time without handcuffs impeding their hug. The three of us then wrapped arms around each other in a circle and thanked God for his love. What else could level the ground in such a profound way that one of the great Christian leaders of our time, a death-row inmate, and a Christian songwriter could come together before the throne of the living God as brothers, one in Christ?

This first trip proved to be one of the most profound experiences of the awesome reality of God's grace I have ever encountered. It also helped me further define the kind of men and women who I want to follow as they follow Christ. The events of that day inspired me to write a song called "Free," which was included on my *Signs of Life* album. Knowing Chuck and getting to visit many correctional institutions since that first visit only deepen my desire for God to free my heart to love all men as he loves me in his Son.

Free

The sun was beating down inside the walls of stone and
    razor wire
As we made our way across the prison yard
I felt my heart begin to race as we drew nearer to the place
Where they say that death is waiting in the dark
The slamming doors of iron echoed through the halls
Where despair holds life within its cruel claws
But then I met a man whose face seemed so strangely out of
    place
A blinding light of hope was shining in his eyes
And with repentance in his voice he told me of his tragic
    choice
That led him to this place where he must pay the price
But then his voice grew strong as he began to tell
About the One he said had rescued him from hell, he said—

I'm free, yeah, oh, I have been forgiven
God's love has taken off my chains and given me these
    wings
And I'm free, yeah, and the freedom I've been given
Is something that not even death can take away from me
Because I'm free
Jesus set me free

We said a prayer and said good-bye and tears began to fill
    my eyes
As I stepped back out into the blinding sun
And even as I drove away I found that I could not escape

The way he spoke of what the grace of God had done
I thought about how sin had sentenced us to die
And how God gave His only Son so you and I could say—

And if the Son has set you free,
Oh, if the Son has set you free
Then you are free indeed,
Oh, you are really free
If the Son has set you free,
Oh, if the Son has set you free
Then you are free, really, really, free

Oh, we're free, yeah, oh, we have been forgiven
God's grace has broken every chain and given us these
    wings
And we're free, yeah, yeah, and the freedom we've been
    given
Is something that not even death can take from you and me
Because we're free, yeah, the freedom we've been given
Is something that not even death can take from you and me
Because we're free, oh, we're free
We are free, we are free
The Son has set us free

If the Son has set you free
You are free indeed

A Road Map for the Journey

Though I will only meet Oswald Chambers in heaven, his writings have given me a tremendous understanding of the life of faith as we journey there. Through his devotional writings, such as *My Utmost for His Highest* and his biography, I gain an image of a life "abandoned to God." His admonition to his fellow workers in the gospel to make an intimate relationship with God the beginning and ending of any ministry continues to prod my heart on to greater passion and consuming love for God. For instance, consider these words of his, called "The Embrace of Love":

> My relationship to God embraces every faculty, I am to love Him with *all* my heart, *all* my soul, *all* my mind, and *all* my strength, every detail is instinct with devotion to Him; if it is not I am disjointed somewhere. Think what you do for someone you love! The most amazing minute details are perfectly transfigured because your whole nature is embraced, not one faculty only. You don't love a person with your heart and leave the rest of your nature out, you love with your whole being, from the crown of the head to the sole of the foot. That is the attitude of the New Testament all through.[1]

I had the distinct privilege of visiting with Oswald Chambers' daughter, Kathleen, when I was recording in London a while back. Since he had died when she was only three years old, most of her memories of him came through her mom. I was invited to her home for tea, where she shared her spirited opinions about everything from how little she likes the contemporary translations of her dad's work to how embarrassed her father would be over all of the "hubbub and fuss made over him" by Christians today.

She also showed me some of her father's original artwork, which deepened my sense of connection with him as a fellow artist. After our afternoon tea, I returned to the studio. Within ten days, Kathleen had joined her dad in heaven.

For Us, to Live Is Christ

Along with Oswald Chambers, I recognize other "mentors from afar" who are in my personal "faith hall of fame." These men and women of God have deeply affected the way I understand the life of grace and faith, and I encourage anyone to get their books and study their lives. These believers have helped me understand what Paul meant when he said, "For to me, to live is Christ and to die is gain" (Phil. 1:21).

A. W. Tozer showed me what it means to "pant after God," to hunger and thirst for God in a way that says, "Feed me, Father, or I die. Slake my thirst or I will perish." He could say more in three pages than most of us can say in thirty.

Corrie ten Boom gave me a vision of "the simplicity and purity of devotion to Christ." Her story, told in the best-seller *The Hiding Place,* did a lot more than inspire me to write a song with the same title. The reality of her struggle to trust Jesus and to stay tender in the cruelest and most degrading of circumstances assaults my complaining spirit.

Dietrich Bonhoeffer's challenging book *The Cost of Discipleship* has helped me understand the difference between cheap grace and transforming grace, and the difference between being in a "discipleship group" and being a disciple of Jesus. Driven by his commitment to ultimate peace, this Christian servant decided to help overthrow Hitler and his evil regime. It cost him his life. Such sacrifice in the face of evil confronts my complacency.

Jim Elliot's brief and passionate life, retold by his wife, Elisabeth, in *Through Gates of Splendor,* makes me continue to ponder what God must do in the heart of a man or woman to give them such joy and willingness to "abandon it all for the sake of the call."

All four of these mentors have a redemptively disturbing presence in my life. They continue to unsettle my status quo notions of what it means to have a relationship with Jesus and to experience his grace.

Choosing the Best

Finally, here are a few tips on choosing your own best mentors:

1. Be intentional about being a follower of Jesus Christ. To have a mentor in songwriting, gardening, and golf is one thing, but to have a mentor in the gospel is quite another. Jesus calls us to be mastered by his cross, not to have our own personal guru or coach. Pray for spiritual mentors who find joy in connecting you to Christ and not primarily to themselves. Look for those who are themselves still in the process of growing in grace as opposed to being "retired from active duty."

2. Be sobered by the fact that each of us is already shaping the lives of those who are watching and following us. We are *all* mentors

117

for others. Therefore, let us be careful about who *we* follow. Our models and mentors are already affecting the generation behind us.

3. Get ready to be taught, exposed, stretched, rebuked, and loved. Don't think primarily about showing up at Starbucks for a latte, a scone, and a deep conversation about your favorite author. Though being an apprentice in the gospel is free, that doesn't mean it won't cost you. To what are you willing to say no in order to say yes to the freedom for which Jesus has set you free?

4. Be realistic. Don't expect to find "the mentor of your dreams." Few of us ever have that experience. Our role models in the faith should be men and women who have lived before us in such a way as to say, "Follow me as I follow Christ." Their lives are a contagion of grace, an aroma of love, an incarnation of the life of the cross, a picture of what it means to suffer well. But many of them may only be accessible to us through great literature, both in Scripture and in thousands of books. But accessible they are. The writer of the book of Hebrews encouraged Christians in his day to take heart from "the great crowd of witnesses" that surrounded them, referring to the Old Testament saints who have left us a living hope in what has been and what is to come. Those same witnesses surround *us*.

5. Choose childlike servants rather than so-called experts as your models. We live in a day when true heroism has been replaced with celebrity. Entertainers and athletes are our culture's heroes. Look for models and mentors who live close to Jesus—those who prefer anonymity to the spotlight; who lovingly take up a towel to wash feet; who are astonished that Jesus loves someone like them. You will find these individuals everywhere.

Scotty:

To reflect on the lives of those the Lord has brought into my life as agents of grace is humbling. They are the kind of men and women who make me hunger for a bread not of this world and thirst for a water that only Jesus can give.

God first became more than a cultural icon to me through my maternal grandparents, Granny and Paw Paw Ward. In their lives, I saw the grace of God years before I ever heard the phrase. Author Eugene Peterson once asked, "Who are the people who have made a difference in my life? Answer: The ones who weren't trying to make a difference."[2] My grandparents were that kind. The only pressure I felt from them was that of their incredible example.

I remember their home in Charlotte, North Carolina, where, as a child, I would spend a week each summer. The highlight of each day was breakfast. My grandmother loved to cook, and her first meal of the day always included freshly churned butter spread over thick toast with a big dollop of homemade fig preserves. My mouth still waters forty years later! But what made the deepest impression on me was not her preserves but her prayers. Granny *showed* me that God is real.

After breakfast, Granny and Paw Paw would each take a Bible-verse card out of a little plastic loaf of bread, give one to each grand-child, and then we would read them in turn. My grandparents then prayed for all their children and grandchildren, one by one. Tears would flow. Granny wept with such tenderness, longing, and grati-tude before God.

At the time, I didn't understand why talking to God would move someone so deeply. All I knew was that I felt deeply loved when I watched them commune with God. If human intercession brings us to faith, then Granny and Paw Paw prayed me into the kingdom. Their seventy-two years of marriage saw almost unbearable pain and suffering through which God alone could sustain them. My grand-father suffered painful depression, and one of their daughters had a heroin addiction for ten years.

God Is All You Need When God Is All You Have

Agnes Lee—dear "Agie"—served as our family cook, cleaner, and resident sage for ten years during my childhood. I could never list my mentors in the faith without mentioning this brave woman. As a young child, I didn't understand why Agie couldn't go to the same restaurants my family did or even drink from the same water fountain. I never heard her complain, but I am sure that a pain filled her soul to which I am a stranger. Yet she gave me a glimpse of a different fountain, the river of God's grace, which has always been open to any who are thirsty, irrespective of skin color.

"Scotty, dear child, it's gonna be all right. God'll take care of you. You can trust him." She spoke these words to me after my mom's death. While other well-wishers offered well-worn clichés, Agie's words were born out of her own sense of abandonment to God. He was all she had. I wish I had taken her more seriously as a child. This woman loved me as her own. Though poor, she made many rich. She planted seeds in my heart that came to harvest long after she died.

God's Word Is True: Love the Bible and Learning

As the wild director of youth ministries for the Burlington YMCA, Joseph Lewis Williams III—alias "JL"—was fresh out of seminary and full of passion and the Holy Spirit. As soon as I became a Christian in 1968, JL invited me to my first Bible study group as a senior in high school. "Turn in your Bibles to the gospel of John," JL said to a roomful of my friends gathered in his home. Embarrassed, not knowing John from Jonah, I fanned myself with the pages of my first Bible as I looked for our text. Within six months of that night, I experienced an inward call by God's Spirit to the ministry of the Word. God has quite a sense of humor!

"So you guys are goin' to Mexico with me this summer?" JL asked one time. "Good, here are thirty-five Scriptures I want you to memorize before you step foot on that bus!" He was preparing twenty-nine young converts not just for our first summer missions trip but also for life.

During our trip to Mexico, for instance, we were exposed to many scenes that distressed me as a baby Christian. At the Shrine of Guadeloupe in Mexico City I watched a long line of older men and women crawl on their raw and bleeding knees on a brick road for a quarter of a mile toward the huge cathedral. *What's going on?* I thought. It made me feel sad. Did this impress God? Did it make him love these believers more? Why did these dear people all look so full of doubt and fear?

JL didn't miss a beat. That evening as we gathered together to discuss the day's events, he asked, "What do you think, guys? How'd you feel watching all those people crawling on their knees? Do they know the Lord better than you? Turn to Ephesians 2:8–10—it's one of the passages you had to memorize to get here!"

Tenderly and powerfully, JL reminded us of the difference between salvation by works and salvation by grace. "What is Paul saying here? It is by *grace*, not by works that we gain a relationship with God. You guys know this, but you can't know it too well. There is *nothing* that we can do to earn a relationship with God, *nothing*! It's not our bleeding knees but Jesus' death upon the cross that relates us to God." There was something about the context of real life and traveling in community that made those early Bible studies so powerful in my life.

When we returned from Mexico, none of us wanted to stop meeting, so the "Y-Teen Caravan" became "The New Directions," an interracial contemporary youth choir that provided me with mentoring through my four years at the University of North Carolina.

JL's mentoring took on a new dimension when he told me one day, "Scotty, a reading Christian is a growing Christian." He gave me a love for great books and learning. Wherever we went in our travels, JL would always sit in the front row with a legal pad in hand, taking notes from *whoever* was teaching or preaching. He modeled an insatiable hunger for truth.

"Scotty, take these guys with you to Carolina this fall." And he handed me a pile of books. Through JL's influence, C. S. Lewis, Francis Schaeffer, and John Stott became mentors of mine. Though he died years before I ever picked up a copy of *Mere Christianity*, C. S. Lewis helped me know that being a Christian does not mean you commit intellectual hara-kiri. Later, through his book *A Grief Observed,* Lewis freed me to grieve the death of my mom. With *The Chronicles of Narnia,* he liberated my imagination from the dungeon of television.

When I decided to major in religion at UNC, JL made sure that Francis Schaeffer walked me through the morass of postmodern and post-Christian thinking that vied for my young Christian mind at the time. Dr. Schaeffer helped me to see *The God Who Is There* in the midst of my liberal and spiritually intense education, where it became increasingly obvious that my '60s culture was trying to *Escape from Reason*. Through his writings and tapes I began to build a genuinely biblical worldview. He helped me understand what *True Spirituality* actually looks like in light of the Fall and in light of the longed for return of Jesus.

When I was so confused about charismatic theology, JL gave me the first edition of John Stott's *Baptism and Fullness*, a study of the Pentecostal teaching on the baptism and gifts of the Holy Spirit of the late '60s and '70s. Through this one book, Stott went on to become my mentor par excellence in Bible study and careful exposition. If Dean Smith is the Michelangelo of college basketball, then John Stott is the Michelangelo of biblical teaching and application. For thirty years he has demonstrated to me how to rightly "divide the word of truth." I own more of his books than of any other single author.

God's Gospel Is So Much Bigger and Glorious Than You Can Imagine

In January 1975, I was just beginning my seminary training at Westminster Theological Seminary, outside of Philadelphia. I had a piece of paper in my hand that said that I had been assigned to a certain C. John Miller, professor of practical theology, as my faculty advisor. I had absolutely no idea who he was. In fact, I remember being disappointed that I wasn't given one of the more well-known faculty members, some heavyweight from the systematic theology department. As I made my way up to his little office at the top of Machen Hall, I didn't know what to expect.

I politely knocked. The door opened not simply to his office but to the heart of a man who taught me more about God, grace, and life than all others combined. "Come in, Scott," he said with a rich and tender voice. Though Jack stood shoulder height to me, he towered above me in every other way.

For the next forty minutes, we got to know each other and discussed my graduate school experience. I don't remember many specifics of our conversation, but I will never forget the last thing he said: "Let's pray, Scott." As soon as he started to pray, I said to myself, this is why God brought me here. He spoke to the Father with an intimacy, reverence, and joy that made me want to both prostrate myself and dance before the Lord! It was a feast of grace. I prayed, *I want to know this man better*—and that's one prayer God has answered beyond my wildest expectations. For the next twenty-one years, Jack Miller loved me as his son.

Jack's greatest contribution to my life concerns the glory and centrality of the gospel. I came into his life at a time when he could say with fresh passion, "I consider my life worth nothing to me, if only I may finish the race and complete the task the Lord Jesus has given me—the task of testifying to the gospel of God's grace" (Acts 20:24). Jack believed that the gospel is the most important message in all of history and also the only essential message in all of history.

"Like Luther, I'm going to beat 'justification by grace through faith' into your heads until you get it!" he told a class one time with a smile and laugh I will never forget. "The biggest problem I encounter in the church today is Christians who are full of fear and unbelief. They have no joy or power. They simply don't believe the gospel. That's their problem! Your knowledge of God is only as valid as your grasp of his gospel," he used to remind us.

Though I came into seminary believing that salvation is by grace and not by works, I wasn't *really* sure what that meant. The main peace I had came from knowing I could never earn salvation. Beyond that, things were pretty muddled. My understanding of salvation looked something like this: When you accept Jesus as your personal Savior, your sins are forgiven, the slate is wiped clean. God puts his Spirit in you and gives you power over temptation and power to please him. As you obey God, you prove that you are born again and can live with the good hope of going to heaven when you die.

I suppose this version of the gospel would sound like good news to a man with no hope, but it is woefully less than the gospel that is revealed in the Scriptures. If *bad* theology is the worst of all taskmasters, then *true* theology is the greatest of all loving masters! This is especially true when it comes to the gospel. Jack took me from skiing on the bunny slope of the gospel to the top of the mountain, to the rarefied air and winding trails of the unsearchable riches of God's grace. It's a lot more dangerous but so much more glorious! Who wants to hold on to a towrope when the chairlift of grace will take us into the peaks of God's love?

God's Children Serve Him Best in Weakness and Brokenness

"Why does ministry have to be so hard?" I asked myself once in despair. I hardly formed the question before the phone rang. "Hello, Scotty, it's Jack." Many times he had called me before, at just the right moment, just when the Spirit of God needed to do a humbling work in my life. But this call, and those that followed, were different. "Scotty, we need each other right now. Both of us need bread from our Father."

During a routine visit to his physician in the fall of 1987 a rapidly growing cancerous tumor was discovered in Jack's abdomen. He heard those dreaded words, "You have lymphoma." The tumor, the size of a cantaloupe, had started to put incredible pressure on his kidneys, which began to fail. The cardiologist was concerned about Jack's heart, which had already survived a heart attack while Jack was preaching in Uganda. Chemotherapy and the prayers of God's people around the world significantly reduced the size of the tumor, but Jack felt weak and frail. So how did it happen that from his position of utter weakness, *he* ministered to *me* in such a powerful way?

I remember his calling me from his hospital bed. "Scotty, I've been meditating on First John 4:16: 'We know and rely on the love God has for us.' I'm staggered at the enormity of God's love for me in this bed. Will you pray for me, that my love for him will increase? Pray that I will be a good witness of his love to all the nurses and people that come in and out of my room." As much as Jack taught me in the classroom, he taught me so much more in his suffering.

Another time during his bout with cancer he called me. "Scotty, I've been watching TV this morning. While flipping around, I came upon Jimmy Swaggart." I fully expected Jack to start lamenting about poor theology, theatrics, and manipulated people. Much to my surprise and shame, he continued, ". . . and here's what the Lord taught me through him." (I thought, *What could the Lord possibly teach a man who was a distinguished professor at Westminster Theological Seminary?*) Jack continued, "As Jimmy Swaggart read from Romans, God spoke to my heart, reminding me that *nothing* will ever separate us from his love. Isn't that wonderful, Scotty?" The curtains of my arrogant soul were thrown open again and exposed to the bright rays of God's grace.

Gracious Gypsies

A year later, after regaining some physical strength, Jack called me with a wild request. "Scotty, what are you and Darlene doing in September?"

"I don't know . . . what do you have in mind, Jack?"

I did a double take when he responded, "I was thinking about us going to southern Spain to witness to Gypsies." Jack believed that the gospel could change anyone anywhere anytime. His vision of the kingdom led him to take what he called "gospel risks." One of his favorite expressions was, "Risk or rust." Jack never rusted!

So we flew to Malaga, in southern Spain, on the Mediterranean. What a ragtag bunch we were! Ten of us, all invited by Jack, were there to learn how God loves to use "the foolish things, the lowly things of this world" (1 Cor. 1:27–28). We qualified. We went to two different Gypsy camps armed with an old flannel graph, a meager skit, little Spanish, and a man who believed in the irresistible power of the gospel. At least King David had a backup army when he took his sling and pebbles into battle with Goliath!

The first camp looked like a low-rent housing project in any big city in America. There we shared the gospel mostly with children, whose intrigue with these Americans gave way to sincere interest in the story of Jesus and his love. The second camp looked more like a scene from the slums of Calcutta. Three square miles of cardboard, rotting plywood, and tin houses! The living conditions were almost inconceivable.

What did it feel like as we stood there in a Gypsy camp, singing hymns in an attempt to gather a crowd? On one hand, I felt foolish, self-conscious, glad that nobody had a video camera! And afraid. As we sang our up-tempo hymns, a couple of Gypsies tried to dance with two of the women with us. Stereotypes of Gypsies filled my imagination, and I briefly wondered if a kidnapping was being set up. Fortunately, a Venezuelan pastor who was with us intervened and drew me into a good-hearted discussion off to the side.

On the other hand, joy began to well up inside of me—and a glimmer of freedom. *Maybe this is what it means to be as a child before Jesus and the world,* I thought to myself. As I watched Jack preach in his broken Spanish, I saw the love that propelled his whole being. He was a dying man preaching to dying men, women, and children. I envied his freedom. I never knew a freer man in all of my life—free from fear, free from living for the approval of others, free to be weak, free to be broken, free to die.

As darkness began to fall, we had one more stop to make. The Venezuelan pastor wanted to take us to a Gypsy church. As we followed him in our cars, I had in my mind images of a wagon caravan circled around a blazing campfire, while dozens of red-bandanna-clad Gypsies danced and banged on tambourines. So when we walked into a neat cinder-block building filled with "normal" looking people, another of my stereotypes was obliterated.

For the next two hours, we sang, listened to testimonies from our Gypsy friends, and beheld the transforming power of the gospel. I finally began to understand what Jack meant when he said, "The gospel can change anybody, anywhere, at any time." Later that night, as we enjoyed our usual 10:00 P.M. supper (the Spanish eat late and long!), a young man came to our table selling flowers. He gave each of the women a small bouquet. When we reached into our pockets to pay him, he refused. "No, no, no! You have already enriched my life by fellowshipping with me in the Lord tonight." This young man, who made his living by selling flowers, was a member of the church we had just attended. His generosity praised the God of all grace.

Live Expectantly, Love the "Little People"

A couple years later, Jack took a group of us to London for a series of prayer walks through a region called Southhall, an area densely populated by families from India. He had a growing burden to plant a church among the Indian population as a way of ultimately sharing the gospel of God's grace with millions of unreached people. On one of the days allotted to tourist interests, we chartered a tour bus to drive our group around London. The whole day, Jack sat on the steps at the front of the bus chitchatting with our English bus driver. We debated among ourselves about where to visit, trying to cram in as many castles and cathedrals as we could. It was a *full* day. We left at 7:00 A.M. and didn't return to our lodging until 7:00 P.M. When we arrived, Jack and the bus driver had disappeared. Fifteen minutes later, they returned—as brothers in Christ. Jack had led him to the Lord. While we were loving being typical tourists, Jack was simply loving.

The last time I was with Jack was about a year before he went to be with the Lord. He and Rose Marie, his wife, stayed in our home while they led a "Sonship" week. "Sonship" is a discipleship course written by Jack and Rose Marie Miller which is built on the foundation of the doctrine of our adoption in Christ. The idea is, as J. I. Packer says, that "Father" is the distinctive Christian name for God. In essence, a "Sonship" week is a weeklong seminar which helps believers come alive to a life of God's grace and the freedom and power of knowing ourselves to be beloved sons and daughters of God. At that time, Jack was still planning to preach in new places. "Scotty, can you go with me to Hamburg, Germany, next January? We have a great opportunity to help our friends understand the difference between legalism and grace in a very strategic German church." My schedule simply would not allow it, but I promised Jack that I would make a follow-up trip.

How I regret my decision, for it was Jack's last preaching mission. He died a couple of months later, after open-heart surgery in Spain. When the heart surgeon opened his chest cavity he was astonished to see that Jack had been living with only about forty percent of his heart muscle still functioning. A heart attack in Uganda and the chemotherapy from his cancer had taken their toll. I believe it was simply his heart for God that kept him so alive during those last years.

Before the "Sonship" conference was over, I was given one lasting image of Jack that, for me, sums up his whole life. One night during that week, I burst into his room in our home without knocking. There I found him on his knees before his open Bible with his hands raised in worship. Oh, how he loved his Father! Jack was the same man even when nobody was watching.

chapter seven

[THAT'S WHAT FRIENDS ARE FOR]

When You Are a Soldier

When you are a soldier I will be your shield
I will go with you into the battlefield
And when your arrows start to fly
Take my hand and hold on tight
I will be your shield, 'cause I know how it feels
When you are a soldier
When you're tired from running
I will cheer you on
Look beside you and you'll see you're not alone
And when your strength is all but gone
I'll carry you until you're strong
And I will be your shield 'cause I know how it feels
When you're a soldier

I will be the one you can cry your songs to
My eyes will share your tears
And I'll be your friend if you win
Or if you're defeated
Whenever you need me I will be here
When you're lost in darkness I will hold the light
I will help you find your way through the night
I'll remind you of the truth
And keep the flame alive in you
And I will be your shield
'Cause I know how it feels
When you are a soldier

Steven:

Friendship—the word conveys many different images. For men, all too often, ballgames, business, and brawn define the boundaries of our friendships. We love our buddies—and, on deeper levels, avoid them. We serve each other and fail each other. One minute we are intimate allies, the next distant strangers.

So what difference does God's grace make in a friendship? All the difference in the world! Jesus' friendship with us should be the paradigm for all our relationships. "My command is this," said Jesus. "Love each other as I have loved you. Greater love has no one than this, that he lay down his life for his friends. . . . I no longer call you servants. . . . I have called you friends" (John 15:12–15).

As we meditate upon Jesus' friendship with us—the great love he has lavished on us in the gospel—a change begins to occur in our hearts. Rather than using people for personal fulfillment, we begin to serve them as objects of God's great affection. We love others as Jesus loves us. Grace extended to us becomes grace extended through us. Mercy showered upon us becomes mercy given to those who fail and disappoint us. Forgiveness from Jesus becomes the means by which we forgive those who hurt us and sin against us.

Pastor David Hansen writes of Jesus' paradigm of friendship,

> The New Testament corroborates that Jesus was a friend to sinners. He visited with them on the streets, called them as disciples, attended their parties and invited himself over to their houses for dinner. In friendship Jesus shared the gospel. Jesus' friendship with sinners was an "enacted parable expressing his message that God made himself the Friend of sinners." When Jesus befriended sinners, they followed him. When the disciples befriended sinners, they followed Jesus. When the "enacted parable" of Jesus' life of friendship was taken over by his disciples they became enacted parables of Jesus. Jesus fully intended his disciples to spend the rest of their lives befriending sinners.[1]

Such is the nature of grace.

I would like to list some people—"enacted parables"—who have given me friendship and shown me "God's grace in its various forms" (1 Peter 4:10). One of the most difficult aspects of writing this chapter is having to limit the number of friends I can include. I am not saying these friends "made the cut" or are my *favorite* friends. Rather, I have chosen from among many faithful men and women who represent different dimensions of the friendship that Jesus offers each of us.

Scotty Smith

Over the last twelve years, Scotty has been a mentor, counselor, confidant, coach, brother, cheerleader, and, most importantly, friend. In their book *Friends and Friendship,* Jerry and Mary White offer this definition: "A friend is a trusted confidant to whom I am mutually drawn as a companion and an ally, whose love for me is not dependent on my performance, and whose influence draws me closer to God."[2] This captures the essence of my friendship with Scotty.

I consider it one of God's greatest gifts to have been able to sit under Scotty's teaching. Many of my best song ideas come from his sermons. (Don't worry, I've already confessed, and he's given me his blessing!) But more precious to me than his teaching has been the relationship we have cultivated through the shared joys and hardships on the journey of grace.

Our friendship started with a phone call. One day shortly after my *For the Sake of the Call* album was released, I picked up the phone. "Is Steven there?" asked the voice on the line. "This is Scotty Smith." At the time Mary Beth and I had visited Christ Community Church a couple of times and had heard Scotty preach, but we were attending another church in a different part of town.

Scotty Smith, calling for me? Wow! To me, this was like a phone call from Billy Graham. As it turned out, he had just listened to my new album and was calling me to say how encouraged he was by it. Needless to say, his call brought me great encouragement as well. I was in the process of writing some Bible study material with my then current pastor, Al Henson, to accompany the record and to use as a follow-up tool for my concert ministry. I called Scotty and asked if we could get together and discuss the content of this study booklet, to be called *The Call*.

I went to meet with Scotty for the first time, prepared to appear spiritually deep and profound. I didn't want to waste the time of this man, known for his knowledge and wisdom, and, to be completely honest, I didn't want him to see what kind of spiritual pigmy I really was. But God and Scotty would not let me get away with my little scheme.

By the time I walked out of Scotty's office that day, we had gone way below the waterline of my prepared agenda. As I started to become more vulnerable about things not at all related to my booklet, I found in Scotty a friend who was willing to be vulnerable with me as well. Together we found ourselves face-to-face with our desperate need not merely for answers to our questions but for a Savior who would love us and change us.

What has characterized our friendship since that first visit? A couple of invaluable features stand out. First of all, we are committed to ask each other important questions. Scotty asked me one such question many years ago that we *continue* to wrestle with over and over, as we never seem to reach closure. "Steven, what is the difference between living a driven life and a called life?" That question haunts us as much as it invites us to reflect on lifestyle issues.

Both of us have far more opportunities to "be busy for Jesus" than we have time or energy to accomplish. But where's the balance? How do the demands of the kingdom of God and the demands of being family men fit together? Is the need the call? What does it means to live for the praise of God and not for the approval of man? How can we stay aware of the barrenness of busyness? How do you know what to say yes to and no to? There are no easy answers to these questions, but when these questions are not being asked, a train wreck is close by.

Secondly, we give each other the freedom to be honest about the different feelings we have when we are not in the public spotlight of professional ministry. Twila Paris once wrote a powerful song entitled

"The Warrior Is a Child." It talks about the confusion, doubts, and fears that God's servants sometimes have when no one is watching. There are a whole lot of people under the influence of our vocations who seem to assume that we must have an incredible relationship with God, one that makes us impervious to the normal struggles of most people. That simply is not true. Our friendship is a place where each of us can admit how overwhelmed we get—how sometimes we feel so unworthy of having so many people's appreciation and affirmation (by the way, that's not all we get!)—how it would be so much easier and better to do anything else than what our callings seem to require of us. While resisting "pity parties," we do not resist being real about how difficult life can be. An understanding heart in a listening friend is a rare gift. We treasure this part of our friendship.

Geoff Moore

My friendship with Geoff was formed out of my need. Geoff and I were brought together by our publisher, who wanted us to cowrite a song. I had heard Geoff sing before, and he had heard some of my songs, but this would be our first meeting. While we emerged from our four hours together with a song that would later be recorded by the country-gospel group Dixie Melody Boys, we also formed the beginning of a friendship. Since that time we have continued to co-write songs for each other's albums and have enjoyed performing together in various settings.

Geoff and his wife, Jan, had been married about six months longer than Mary Beth and I, newlyweds at the time. Assuming that Geoff must have had this marriage business all figured out, I began to pour out my heart to him concerning some of the struggles Mary Beth and I were having. But rather than finding him to be the master of marriage (I can hear Jan chuckling even as I write this), I discovered a friend who was willing to be vulnerable, to listen, and to fight the good fight alongside me. Since that first visit, we have shared many times together and laughed ourselves silly. We've wrestled with our callings as dads, husbands, artists, and colleagues in ministry.

Geoff fulfills the role Gordon MacDonald refers to as "a special friend":

> Special friends are part of the economy of spiritual passion, and in most cases an indispensable part. Unlike the very draining and the very nice people of our worlds, special friends are committed to helping one another discover and maintain spiritual passion. Each member of a team of special friends rejoices when another succeeds. Each weeps when another falls. Special friends do not envy when someone wins; nor do they gloat at failure.[3]

Early on in our friendship, Geoff noticed how hard it was for me simply to have fun. My wife and I now refer to Geoff as "a party looking for a place to happen." My earlier struggles with legalism had made it hard for me to relax and enjoy innocent pleasures. I still remember the day that Geoff said to me in the presence of our wives, "One of my goals in this life is to teach Steven Curtis Chapman how to have fun." I am glad to say that he has been faithful to that goal. We have fished for salmon together in the rivers of Alaska and have ridden Harleys in the snow-topped mountains of the Colorado Rockies. Geoff has opened my eyes and heart to the glories of God's creation and the good news that he "has given us all things freely to enjoy."

A Circle of Friends—A Circle of Hope

It was a typical small-group get-together for a typical small group—old friends and new in the early stages of trying to jell as a group. The things we shared were sincere but safe. Five couples and our kids—Mary Beth and I, Ray and Lori Mullican, Mike and Rhinda Smith, and Dan and Terri Coley—members of the same church and neighbors, all wanting to develop some consistent fellowship with a few friends.

On January 2, 1998, we gathered at the Coley's to watch the University of Tennessee play for the national championship. While we guys were enthralled with the game, our kids were rolling around on the floor, giggling, and having a great time. Our wives had varying levels of interest in the game but enjoyed the event, chatting with each other and keeping the snack foods coming.

At halftime Mary Beth suggested we go home since she wasn't feeling well. As we rounded up our three children, Ray and Lori were having the same discussion. "Ray, I think we better go too. Alex and Erin need to get to bed before too long."

"Honey, I'd love to stay and watch the rest of the game, but I want us to all be together." Mary Beth remembers overhearing their conversation that ended with Ray almost reluctantly sending his family on home without him.

"Mom, can I stay with Daddy?" Erin, the Mullican's almost-nine-year-old daughter pleaded. They discussed it for a moment but then arrived at the decision that Erin should go on with her mom and her sister.

About an hour after we got home, the call came. There had been a horrible wreck. While crossing a stoplighted intersection, Lori, Alex, and Erin had been broadsided by a young man who ran the light. The only message we received was that things were serious. There was the possibility that the crash had been fatal.

I got in my car and made tracks for the hospital. My cellular phone rang. It was Mary Beth. "Steven, Erin didn't make it."

That short but tragic announcement literally left me speechless. I thought, *This can't be true. Surely, there's some mistake. Erin was just rolling around on the floor at the Coleys' with my kids just an hour ago.*

At times we had some deep discussions about pretty weighty issues we were dealing with, mixed in with the usual small-group dialogue revolving around the typical hassles of life, but nothing like this—now we were confronting death together, one of our own, one of our kids.

How do newly bonding friends walk together in profound grief? What prepares us for funerals of little girls who die one week short of their ninth birthday? What do you say and not say to parents who have had their hearts ripped out by such a tragedy?

In the weeks following Erin's funeral, God began to work in ways that are new to me. It was as though her death was this huge boulder

135

of providence that God hurled into the rather placid waters of our small group. The rippling effect, however, has continued to send out waves of grace, not waves of bitterness. It is hard to describe the miracle of God's love that we have shared together and the lessons we have been learning about true friendship.

One Sunday night a few months later, our small group met again. We had grown now with the addition of Al and Nita Andrews, a couple who had been friends with the Mullicans for several years, and Mike and Cady Wilson. That night, Al, who had become our "leader," began, "Tonight let's talk about hope. What does it really look like? What do you hope for? What does it mean to hope in the face of tragedy?" Al asked us. "A tragedy like Erin's death.... What are our options? We can either kill hope, abandon hope, or let it grow. How will we choose?"

As he spoke, I couldn't help but think about my experience a few months earlier of being a part of the combined funeral services for three high school girls who were shot and killed after a before-school prayer meeting at Heath High School in Paducah, Kentucky. This tragedy also hit close to home because of the fact that I had grown up in Paducah and had graduated from that same high school seventeen years ago. Never before in my life had I stared such grief in the face as at the funeral services of these three girls—and one month later, at the funeral for Erin.

How do people in the world deal with such senseless events without any basis for hope? It's hard enough for Christians. As our small group continued to meet, we became a circle of hope—friends committed to living out the reality of grace in the tension of the "already and the not yet" of our faith. As we have learned to grieve together as friends, so we have learned to rejoice together in the great truths of the gospel. In fact, it was from these experiences that I wrote the song "With Hope" for the Mullicans, as well as the families of Kacie Stegers, Nicole Hadley, and Jessica James.

With Hope

This is not at all how
We thought it was supposed to be
We had so many plans for you

We had so many dreams
And now you've gone away
And left us with the memories of your smile
And nothing we can say
And nothing we can do
Can take away the pain
The pain of losing you, but—

We can cry with hope
We can say goodbye with hope
'Cause we know our goodbye is not the end, oh no
And we can grieve with hope
'Cause we believe with hope
(There's a place by God's grace)
There's a place where we'll see your face again
We'll see your face again

And never have I known
Anything so hard to understand
And never have I questioned more
The wisdom of God's plan
But through the cloud of tears
I see the Father's smile and say well done
And I imagine you
Where you wanted most to be
Seeing all your dreams come true
'Cause now you're home
And now you're free, and—

We have this hope as an anchor
'Cause we believe that everything
God promised us is true, so—

We wait with hope
And we ache with hope
We hope with hope
We let go with hope

Probably the culminating moment in this whole saga of Erin's death occurred recently as members of our small group gathered with others in a courtroom one year after the collision that took her life. It was time for the young man to face the judge and the consequences of his action. At the attorney's instructions, there had been no interaction between the Mullicans and this young man and his mom. Our church family had been reaching out to them but this would be the first time Ray and Lori would see him. How would they respond? Like any good parents, the Mullicans had gone through seasons of great anger, confusion, hurt, and disbelief. But a year later, what would well up in their hearts?

The judge, obviously sympathetic to Ray and Lori's loss, asked them in front of all of us assembled in the court, "What do you want from me? What kind of punishment do you feel is appropriate in light of your great tragedy?" I could sense that he was willing to administer the full weight of the law if it would in any way help heal the crushed hearts of these parents.

Ray responded, "Your honor, we have prayed and decided to leave this in your hands and, more importantly, in God's hands. We only want what is best for this young man." I had a flashback to the moment when Mary Beth first spoke those words which left me speechless, "Erin didn't make it."

And now I was speechless again, left without words in the presence of such a manifestation of God's grace. I don't think I have ever witnessed a greater demonstration of the power of the gospel. After adjournment, Ray and Lori walked towards the front of the courtroom. I watched them give a sincere and generous embrace to the one who had taken so much from them. I overheard Ray say to him, "We've prayed a lot for you. How can we help?"

Friendship has taken on a whole new depth of meaning for those of us who walked together through "the valley of the shadow of death." Dan and I sat on his front porch one evening reflecting on the journey our small group had been through. We were both mad and sad. "I just want to be different because of this," he said. "How will this make us love our kids and each other differently?"

There is still much pain in Ray and Lori's hearts. How could there not be? But God has knit our hearts together in love. None of us is alone. There are still more tears to be shed and rejoicing to be shared between us, all because the gospel is true.

Mary Beth

It would be impossible to talk about how God reveals his grace to us through friendship without acknowledging my very best friend in the world, my wife. From the first time we met, we've not stopped dreaming together and sharing our hopes, disappointments, questions, laughter, and tears. We've found some wonderful common ground, and we've met each other on the battlefield—because of both, our friendship has become the most precious one I have. Truly, one of the greatest gifts of grace that God has given me in this life, one that leaves me speechless, is my friend and my wife, Mary Beth.

Scotty:

God Prepares a Man for Friendship

The road to friendship has not been easy for me. I've taken many detours. While I treasure my friendship with Steven, it has required time and grace—mostly because I am far more adept at doing things *for* people than walking deeply *with* them. Author Patrick Morley laments, "Most men could recruit six pallbearers, but hardly anyone has a friend he can call at 2:00 A.M."[4] But our Father relentlessly makes relationships the primary issue of our lives, so when we went to Nashville, God used our move to expose the depth of my isolation and invite me into rich community.

One day, still feeling horrible about the Hogan House fiasco, I was flipping through my record collection, looking for something appropriate for those times when I feel like Eeyore, the melancholic donkey in the Winnie the Pooh stories. That night I played a record by British musician John Pantry, who sang one song about friends and friendship. When he reached a line about "the pricelessness of good mates," tears began to spill from my eyes. Something deep inside me longed for release.

Friends! In that painful, sacred moment, I felt the consequences of living life too independently, isolated in a sea of good people who longed to come ashore and be part of my life. I was a man with hundreds of acquaintances but no deep friends, and I could taste my aloneness. Solomon's words described me well: "If one falls down, his friend can help him up. But pity the man who falls and has no one to help him up!" (Eccl. 4:10).

Many people had extended themselves to me. Many had tried to know me. But I had deceived myself early in life with the lie that it is best to be completely self-reliant. I became skilled at manipulating my world to minimize pain and maximize hassle-free living. This principle of "taking responsibility for yourself" coupled with a natural shyness made it easy for me to navigate through life in a one-man rowboat. Fortunately, my little vessel got dashed against the rocks of God's severe mercy.

As I continued to cry, Darlene walked into the room. Without a word, she put her arms around me and just held me. Her tenderness confused me at first. On one hand, it was healing. On the other, it made me want to hide. I had never felt so safe—but unworthy. In seven years of marriage, I hadn't allowed her to get this close, but now, as my reserves suddenly gave out, I simply let her love me.

In the midst of her disappointment about our move, my brokenness represented the first ray of hope for her. She had prayed for the day when my many words would be replaced with many tears. For me to acknowledge that I need others brought Darlene a quiet joy. My idols of stoicism and self-sufficiency had finally begun to fail me, and for the first time in my life, I was ready to have and be a friend.

But I didn't want just any garden-variety friendship. I wanted a friendship built upon the foundation of the grace of God. What follows are the highlights of how God has provided grace-driven friendships when I least deserved or expected them.

Vulnerability, the Vehicle of Grace

Covered only with towels, two men sat in the steam room at a sports club, exhausted from three games of racquetball. We were tired physically, spiritually, and emotionally.

I had met Scott Roley several months before, while still in Winston-Salem. His musical trio, Albrecht, Roley and Moore, had performed at our church as a part of an outreach concert series for students in the community. As we had sat in the church parlor before the performance, something clicked between Scott and me. Although eye contact has always been difficult for me, Scott managed to look through my eyes right down into my heart. For years I referred to it as "deep calling unto deep," although, looking back, "one weary sinner sniffing out another" better describes the attraction!

As only God can time these things, seven months after Scott and I first met, Darlene and I moved to Nashville—where Scott and his wife, Linda, had also recently moved. A couple of weeks later, I called Scott. We decided the safest turf for insecure men is sports or business, so we chose racquetball. How ironic—that was the first and the last time we ever played the game in our twenty years of friendship.

After an hour of swatting the ball around, we retired to the steam room where Scott surprised me with his vulnerability. "If this relationship is going to go anywhere I want to start by letting you know what a mess I am, Scotty. I've done some foolish things with my life." The more he shared *his* problems with me, the freer *my* heart became. His vulnerability became a means of grace for me. While it would have been out of line for two naked men to hug in a steam room, the thought did occur to me.

The domino effect of shared confessions turned that steam room into a sanctuary, a cathedral of grace. Up to that point, both Scott and I feared the words of the psalmist, "My friends and companions avoid me because of my wounds; my neighbors stay far away" (Ps. 38:11). In our case, shared wounds actually cemented our companionship, becoming the means by which we began to experience the love of God in a transforming way. Proverbs teaches, "A friend loves at all times, and a brother is born for adversity" (17:17). To this day, I have found friendship more through the path of shared weakness and pain than any other route.

Twenty years later, our friendship is still maturing. As with vintage wine, a good relationship takes a lot of time and patience before the bouquet can be fully enjoyed. But the gift of a good friendship can become the portal of entry into more. Because of my friendship with Scott, I am learning other lessons about grace-centered friendships.

Acceptance Without Acquiescence

We must become good stewards of vulnerability, however. The freedom to share our "stuff" must lead to the commitment to help each other grow. God loves his children exactly as we are, but he loves us too much to leave us that way.

When the breakthrough to vulnerability occurs in a friendship, it is dangerously easy for two friends to enact a silence that includes a no-hassle clause: "You don't mess with my stuff, and I won't mess with yours. Let's just enjoy being a 'grace cushion' in each other's life." It is at this point that many support groups and friendships end up doing more harm than good. Sometimes sharing an intimate brokenness can be confused with significant relationship. We end up sharing what a mess we are with each other but never talk about the necessity of changing.

When Steven and I began to move beyond casual friendship to a true sharing of our sin and struggles, we had a choice to make. We could either minimize the issues, and thus marginalize our need for God's grace, or we could risk greater exposure and build a friendship committed to helping both of us mature. We have chosen the later.

For instance, one of the defining moments in our relationship occurred in the boardroom of Sparrow Records, Steven's record label. We had gathered as a ministry team to help Steven plan his next season of ministry and tour when he just broke down. "Guys, I don't know how much more I can take." The tears that filled his eyes were just a small indication of the confusion and pain that filled his heart. His sense of hopelessness gave me freedom to identify and acknowledge my own.

I remember being so moved that I got up and embraced Steven and kissed him on the cheek. After the meeting, Steven and I got off in a corner by ourselves. "Steven, I want you to know that my hug a few moments ago says less about my pastoral instinct than it does my own identification with your hurt. I'm feeling exactly what you are. I have never felt so personally weary and ready to bolt."

As we talked, it became obvious that we were both married to women with deep and legitimate longings for intimacy but that neither of us came into marriage with the natural instinct for "loving our wives as Christ loved the church." The easiest thing in the world has been for us to provide financially for our families. But loving our wives and families demands a whole lot more.

It would have been too easy for us simply to sympathize with each other, or to convince ourselves that our wives had unrealistic expectations. We chose, however, to focus on repentance and change, as the gospel requires. We committed to take a serious look at our schedules to help us discern what was essential and what was not—for often, good activities are the enemy of the best. There are always far more opportunities to minister than God's will demands of us.

More importantly, we decided to go to good Christian counselors. Although we are both proud, we are not so proud as to refuse the help offered by gifted men and women with skill to apply the grace of Christ to our foolish hearts. Both Steven and I tend to be overly simplistic and "spiritual" in assessing the crises in our hearts and homes. Grace frees us to humble ourselves and get help! We chose then and continue to choose to "provoke one another to love and good deeds." In a good friendship there will be vulnerability and a shared commitment to change.

To accept someone does not mean acquiescing to their foolishness. Rather, we should offer an embrace that says, "I am going to love you into something better. I'm not going anywhere. You may disappoint and hurt me, but you are not going to shock me or run me off." The foundation for such a relationship must be the gospel. The apostle Paul wrote, "Accept one another, then, just as Christ accepted you, in order to bring praise to God" (Rom. 15:7). Jesus accepts us fully and eternally. He is not going to abandon us or reject us, no matter what. He simply applies more grace and reminds us that our Father is going to bring to completion the good work that he began in us.

Other-Centered Friendship

Through the years I have learned much about grace-empowered friendships by watching my wife and her friends. She tends to have long-term friendships that can weather all kinds of challenges, trials, and heartaches. Most of her friends describe her as a great listener, a nurturer, full of compassion, and committed for the long haul.

Having grown up in a home broken by divorce and alcohol, Darlene has cultivated a heart of mercy for other broken people (which, after all, includes all of us). She is able to put her arms around the whole person, including their struggles. In this, her model is Jesus, who knows us the best, loves us the most. He has promised *never* to leave us or forsake us.

I am deeply challenged by the quality of friendship that Darlene extends to women who have experienced sexual abuse. Since this deep wounding has been a part of her own story, she models for me the way that God comforts us with his mercy and love so that we might share that same comfort with others.

To be a good friend is to know our own weakness, failure, and foolishness well enough to share it with others, with humility and a longing to grow. It is also to anticipate such experiences in every friend that we make. The longer we spend time with *anyone*, the greater the probability that we will be disappointed and disappointing. There is no friend or group of friends in the world who will be able to "fill us up," that is, who will be able to meet the deepest longings of our heart.

I once heard a bad marriage described as a tick-on-a-dog-relationship—but one with no dog and two ticks. The same can be said of a bad friendship. It would be like two friends plugging their umbilical cords into one another expecting and demanding that the other be life for them.

God's grace enables us to serve one another because of the way Jesus serves us in the gospel. We learn to love each other as we are loved by him. Unfortunately, our culture tends to value only those relationships that are personally gratifying. This trend often defines our relationship with God—"What's in it for *me?* I will be as committed to this friendship as I am personally fulfilled and satisfied." Friends, spouses, and churches are chosen and discarded for purely functional reasons.

Recently, I encountered a graphic example of this trend. After I had preached one Sunday, a woman approached me with a lilt in her step and a smile on her face. "Scotty, thank you for giving me permission to divorce my husband today."

After recovering from my shock, I said, "I did what?"

"Well, in your sermon you mentioned how God deeply cares about our joy. I got to thinking about the obstacles to joy in my life— and it hit me. My biggest 'joy robber' is my husband, and since God wants me happy, he obviously is freeing me from that jerk. Thank you for being an instrument of God today!"

Needless to say, we talked further. It is disconcerting to see how Christians live out the narcissism and relativism of our culture. As with fast-food restaurants, we expect relationships to offer us quick service and instant gratification at little cost, and if they fail to deliver, changing friends is no harder than changing restaurants.

Telling Secrets, Not Just Stories

"What's *really* going on, Scotty? I hear what you're saying, but what do you mean?" Mike has always demanded honesty from me. For him, the gospel means truth telling. And for him, friendship, close friendship, means no secrets.

But Mike, in his friendships, is also capable of being honest with himself as well. One day, he asked me, "Can we go for a walk? I've been pondering the death of my dad lately. I still have a lot of anger left over from the days of watching him be consumed with everything but me. Look at this old photograph. That's me lying on the floor next to my dad's bedroom door. I'm trying to talk to him under the door crack. He would come home from work exhausted, go to his room, and bury himself in there. I never knew my mom took this picture until I found a copy of it. Why was that door closed so much of the time? Why did I have to pass notes under the door to communicate with my own dad? I could easily become the very evil I hate."

Each of us has secrets—painful stories that, even though they don't excuse, explain our anger, fears, longings, and ways of relating. Sometimes it takes years to acknowledge them. Memories of childhood sexual abuse, lies we have lived, shame-producing things we've done—we all have secrets, which stay secrets, that is, until the love of God frees us to confess, acknowledge, and begin healing.

Larry Crabb talks about the importance of sharing secrets in his book *The Silence of Adam*:

> Secrets come in several varieties. There are secrets involving *specific events*, memories of things others have done to us, or things we have done. There are secret *internal realities*: urges, interests, struggles, motives, thoughts, beliefs or feelings that we regard as unacceptable, that we think would spoil any relationship in which they were known. Sometimes the things we hide are *vague but powerful impressions*, usually involving an unnamed but terrifying sense of our own despicableness, a sense that—we fear— others would confirm if given the chance.
>
> Secrets have three major effects:
> 1. They weaken *courage*.
> 2. They isolate their keepers from *community*.
> 3. They erode a legitimate sense of *personal confidence*.[5]

Steve Green is another friend who models the freedom of "being known." When Steve and his family decided to make our church their community, he made an appointment with me. "Scotty, as I come under your pastoral care, I want our relationship to be based on truth and grace, so there are some parts of my story I want you to know."

For the next hour, Steve shared his story. It was not about how God launched one of the most respected Christian music ministries, but the story of how one man has struggled and dealt honestly with temptation and sin, and how he was called to walk in the light. We shared our secrets with each other at the beginning of our friendship, and we have continued to have no illusions about one another's need for grace.

Most recently I have walked with Steve through the sometimes painful transition from his singing to auditoriums packed with two or three thousand fans to a different season in his musical career and ministry. Steve is now what is known as a "father" in the contemporary Christian music circles. While that is, indeed, a compliment, it also carries with it the reality of changes, which sometimes mean smaller venues and lower record sales.

I have never admired, loved, and respected my friend more than now, as he adjusts to these changes. Nothing reveals more clearly what is in the heart of a man than when his vocation is threatened, under stress, or changing shape. It can be either a time for struggling in the lonely place of our fears and insecurities or a time of moving into rich relationship with others to share the load.

Instead of looking for "new marketing strategies" or groping for timeworn clichés to explain and spiritualize the process, Steve has simply chosen to deal faithfully with God's sovereignty over his career, family, and life. He is choosing to go deeper into the heart of the gospel as God redefines and redirects his ministry. Right now, among other things, that means being rubbed into the fabric of our community in Franklin, Tennessee, as a man working for the transformation of the culture and community. Steve has become a part of a group of men known as the Empty Hands Fellowship, a group of brothers who gather with empty hands, with no other agenda than laying hold of the reasons that God has laid hold of us with his grace and love.

Our community has a history of being torn by racial strife and religious pride. This group of fifteen or so pastors and laymen, half black and half white, gather twice a week to pray together and worship God.

The openness and vulnerability with which Steve is dealing with this transition invites my own heart to be honest about my own fears as I move into a new season of life and ministry. My next birthday will be my fiftieth! Egad! I thought Jesus would be back by now! By watching, listening, and walking with Steve, I am freed to admit how I can make anything into an idol, including being a pastor of a big church with a lot of cool people in it. Jack Miller's words echo in my heart: "Scotty, be careful. The ministry can be a seductive mistress." I am also freed to trust my Father who does all things well, even when he doesn't choose to do all things easy.

Accountable for What We Believe, Not Just for What We Do

For several years Buddy and I have been accountable to one another as friends and fellow elders in the same church. Like most "accountability groups," ours started out emphasizing a consistent use of spiritual disciplines.

"Scotty, how have your quiet times been? Are you staying in the Word? How much time are you getting in prayer? Do you have any particular sins to confess?" Buddy and I would faithfully ask each other about these matters. They are important questions that represent essential disciplines in the Christian life, and I am so glad that we have cared enough about each other to invest ourselves in the process of spiritual formation.

But we discovered, in time, that a faithful and dutiful practice of spiritual disciplines, without a strong emphasis on the gospel, tends to create proud legalists, just like we were becoming. To give ourselves to the right disciplines without the proper motivation and understanding of grace can be lethal. Confronting this issue in the lives of religious leaders, Jesus said, "Woe to you Pharisees, because you give God a tenth of your mint, rue and all other kinds of garden herbs, but you neglect justice and the love of God. You should have practiced the latter without leaving the former undone" (Luke 11:42). Jesus didn't condemn the discipline of tithing, even that of herbs, but he did condemn tithing with the wrong heart.

As a freshman in college (and a freshman in the faith), I cut nearly a whole week of classes during my first semester to read through the entire New Testament with a yellow marker in hand. My goal wasn't to immerse myself in the Good News of the gospel. I wanted to be able to go to my Campus Crusade for Christ meetings with a marked-up Bible in hand. Those sitting on either side of me would be able to behold the fruit of my disciplined "searching of the Scriptures." What they really beheld was a Pharisee in the making, a disciplined fool whose grades suffered a severe blow that week!

As Buddy and I discover more of God's grace, we are no less faithful to ask each other searching questions and to make each other accountable, but the questions have changed. We are more likely to ask one another, "Are you believing the gospel today? Are you repenting of how little you trust in the love of God? Are you trying to please God today in terms of your own righteousness or that of Jesus? Are you loving well? Are you walking by faith or by your performance? What idols are being exposed in your life through the love of God?"

Walking with Buddy as a partner in grace, I find that our quiet times center more on fellowshipping with our Father than on congratulating ourselves for reading our four chapters of the Bible every day. Prayer is sitting at the feet of Jesus rather than working through a list of requests. Worship is less about going to church than it is panting after the One who alone can slake our deep thirst with his living water. Grace-defined friendships will always expose our weaknesses and drive us to the all-sufficient Jesus.

part three

[GOD'S COMPELLING LOVE]

What do you think happened to the pearl merchant who found the "mother-of-all-pearls" in Jesus' parable? "He went away and sold everything he had and bought it" (Matt. 13:46). The story stops there. We have no idea what happened after he sold his possessions to obtain the treasure. Surely, he found the longing of his heart. This one pearl left him speechless. But how comfortable could he be knowing that he carried his entire estate in his pocket?

When everything you treasure is reduced to one thing, life becomes simple, but new complexities emerge. We, who have exchanged the poverty of our so-called riches for the pearl of God's grace, experience great joy. Certainly. But we soon realize that it is a treasure that cannot be protected in a safety deposit box. No vault in the world can contain it. The pearl of God's love is really a huge boulder hurled into the tranquil pool of our self-centered living. The ripples both upset and liberate us. It's like getting a cute, cuddly lion cub as a pet. Before long, its gentle purring gives way to deafening roars, and its soft baby fur becomes the mane of the king of the jungle! Who owns whom then?

In this final section we invite you to join us in pondering some of the massive implications of the compelling love of God revealed in the gospel.

chapter eight

[FREEDOM TO HURT AND GRIEVE]

Fingerprints of God

> I can see the fingerprints of God
> When I look at you
> I can see the fingerprints of God
> And I know it's true
> you're a masterpiece (work of art)
> That all creation quietly applauds
> You're covered with the
> fingerprints of God
>
> I can see the tears filling your eyes
> And I know where they're coming from
> Coming from a heart that's broken in two
> By what you don't see
> The person in the mirror doesn't look like the mag-
> azine
> but when I look at you it's clear to me
> Just look at you
> A wonder in the making (a wonder of God's own
> making)
> Oh, and God's not through
> In fact, He's just getting started
>
> Never has there been and never again
> will there be another you
> Fashioned by God's hand
> And perfectly planned
> to be just who you are

And what He's been creating
 Since the first beat of your heart
 Is a living breathing priceless
Work of art

Steven:

"Divorce is not in our vocabulary." If I'd heard it once, I'd heard it a thousand times. Ever since my mom and dad recommitted their lives to Christ, they wanted me and Herbie to know that even when times got tough, they were staying together. I believed them. I really did.

They've been divorced now for about eight years. In the after-shock, my soul is just only recently beginning to settle down. The con-flicting emotions, ambivalence, and confusion I experienced were profound. As a Christian, when I stand before thousands of people to proclaim the "peace that passes all understanding," I sometimes feel like a hypocrite, for my own peace was shaken, if not altogether absent at times. How are we to make sense of these moments when every-thing we've been taught to be trustworthy appears otherwise? What do we do when God's promises seem to apply to everyone but us?

My parents' struggle goes back as far as I can remember. I have already shared that I was conceived as a kind of a peace offering, one final attempt to salvage an already shaky marriage. I came into the world as a small mediator, a burden too great for any child to bear, but I gave it my best shot.

My hope grew strong when, at the age of seven, I witnessed my parents give their hearts to God. Theirs was not just an emotional response to some high-powered evangelist. Things actually started to change at home. The bickering and tension were transformed into redemptive communication and caring. Although they still had con-flicts, I could sense the presence of grace in their conflicts, and that meant a lot to me. They learned to "fight fair," and that made me feel secure.

As Mary Beth and I prepared for marriage, we decided to pattern our relationship after theirs. I had memories of my mom following me to the school bus and quoting the promises of God for me; I had images of my dad encouraging me to pray with him over the most basic decisions of life. He even became the minister of music at our church. Mary Beth and I wanted to be like them.

When the rumbling of trouble started to resurface in their marriage, I didn't take it seriously—at first. Unfortunately, it got worse. My dad had assured me, "Steven, we're not going anywhere. We're just working through some issues." I felt the pull as the "peace child" to get in the middle once again. All I knew to do at first was to "stand in the gap," thinking that if I prayed hard enough, certainly God would spare their marriage. I even started soliciting prayer for them at my concerts.

My mom would tell me one side of the story, my dad another. What could I do? Our roles seem to have been reversed—as though I'd become the parent-counselor to two adolescents. Confusion and anguish flourished—these were my spiritual heroes, my models for my own marriage! As the disillusionment and pain began to mount, I wrote a song with my mom in mind called "Waiting for Lightning"— I so wanted something dramatic and supernatural to occur that I got angry at my dad simply because he wouldn't take my mom dancing.

Waiting for Lightning

Standing on the edge of the truth
Looking out at the view of all you used to believe
From where you are you can see you're far away from home
Echoes of the life you once knew call out to you from
    across the divide
And you know it's time to step back over the line But you're
Waiting for lightning—a sign that it's time for a change
And you're listening for thunder while He quietly whispers
    your name

Night falls and the curtain goes down—No one's around
It's just you and the truth as you lie in wait
For a feeling to take you by storm
Somewhere in the depths of your heart where it's empty
    and dark
There's a flicker of light and the Spirit calls
But do you notice at all? Are you . . .

Waiting for lightning—a sign that it's time for a change
And you're listening for thunder while He quietly whispers
  your name

But the sign and the word have already been given
And now it's by faith we must look and we must listen
  instead of
Waiting for lightning—a sign that it's time for a change
And you're listening for thunder while He quietly whispers
  your name

About eight months later, I got the call. Dad said, "Steven, we've signed papers, but don't worry, we're not divorcing. You know how lawyers are. We're just protecting ourselves."

By this time, all I could see was darkness. "My parents have deceived themselves. For thirty years they've used all of the right words, but now look—moms and dads are just grown-up fools."

For the first time, I found rivulets of erosion showing up in my own faith. "They've known God a lot longer than I have—so what's to keep me and Mary Beth from following suit?" We started seeing a counselor because, as we watched their relationship disintegrate, the effects of their misery had come knocking on our own door. Fortunately, we had enough wisdom to seek help. I have watched as too many of my friends have held on to their pride and the illusion that Christians shouldn't have to struggle.

Where am I now? As I have watched, more of the ugly backwash of divorce has crept closer to the most tender places in my heart, the places usually reserved for strong confidence in God. For a long time, I had to deal with the pressure to keep up a "strong witness." So many people look to me to speak the word of faith, to help them through their own crises. I haven't had time for my own heart work.

My earlier faith taught me Bible verses and an image of God that I thought were waterproof. I'm not so sure anymore. I have had to deal with feelings of alienation from God, a certain unfamiliarity with him and his ways. There was a time when I wouldn't have dared to "go there." I would have steered my heart into the safe harbor of predigested answers and stock verses.

But lately I've been thinking about the difference between the way God is supposed to be and the way he really is. Lest this sounds like the musings of a depressed man preparing to embrace agnosticism, please know that there is a work of grace going on in my heart that is giving me the freedom to sit in God's presence without having to know everything or have everything explained to my satisfaction. And in the process, the Bible is becoming more real to me. I can appreciate the deep meaning of the Bible stories—their pathos and power—without having to hunt for a promise to claim or a precept to obey. Job's confusion, Jeremiah's lament, Habakkuk's heartache, Paul's disappointments—I now see that the wilderness is also a part of the story of grace.

Ken Gire writes of this inner wilderness in his book *Windows of the Soul:*

> As physical hunger intensifies with the absence of food, so spiritual hunger intensifies with the absence of God. That is why the wilderness plays such an important role in our lives. . . . Whatever the wilderness, wherever the wilderness, it is in that wilderness where we learn that we do not live by bread alone but by every word that proceeds from the mouth of God, that His word is not only the most natural food for our soul but the most necessary.[1]

Though I can explain some things about what happened to my parents—they got out of fellowship, they started living without spiritual accountability, there was a bitter church split—I know that many painful events are far more complex than that. As the prophet Jeremiah said, "The human heart is deceitfully wicked, more so than anything else. Who can discern it?" I am praying for grace to pursue my parents even as I continue to feel the painful consequences of their choices. It isn't easy, but when is loving ever easy?

Scotty and I are walking through these places together. Both of us have spent a lot of our lives giving other people answers. Frankly, it feels healthy to experience a level of God's grace that brings the freedom to hurt and the opportunity to say, "I'm not really sure about everything." We are finding that God's grace is no mere anesthetic. It is so much more substantive and important than that. The grip of grace is a lot more sure and meaningful than my grasp of the mysteries of God. Is there such a thing as peaceful restlessness?

Scotty:

One Man's Journey Toward Freedom

With our four-week-old daughter nestled close to her heart, my wife stood next to the casket in which her father's body had been laid. He had taken his life. Conflicting feelings—profound sadness, guilt, and confusion over the ways of God, on the one hand, and the great joy of holding her firstborn on the other—coursed through her being. Does God ever expect too much of us? What are we to do with the overwhelming feelings of loss, unfairness, and anger? Is it ever okay to struggle with God's way of doing things?

As days turned into weeks, I watched Darlene's spirits sink lower. With confusion about the eternal state of Christians who commit suicide, my wife's heart reeled with inexpressible feelings and thoughts. What more could she have done? I'd never seen Darlene's faith so severely tested. She'd always been such a rock, so full of confidence in the Lord. Eventually, her feelings began to unnerve me. I wasn't used to doubt or uncertainty. In eight years of being a Christian, four as a married man, I'd never questioned God—about anything. If he said something in his Word, I believed it and that settled it. Negative emotions were not taught in my first discipleship course.

So as Darlene's wrestling with God became more intense and her grief more pronounced, I decided to exercise my spiritual leadership by providing some much-needed counsel: "Honey, I want you to spend more time meditating on Philippians, Paul's book on joy in the Christian life. Don't you think you've been grieving long enough? I know it's been hard, but the Scriptures call us to rejoice in all circumstances, including difficult ones. How have your quiet times been lately, anyway? Seems to me you're playing right into the Devil's schemes. He has only come to rob, kill, and destroy."

That's basically how I responded to her grief. I simply had no other resources to deal with her pain and sadness, and, understandably, Darlene's pain intensified in light of my response. It would be years before I could see that I had related to my wife in a time of deep loss and grief exactly as Job's friends had related to him—with many words and little real presence.

How could I have been so insensitive and uncaring at such a critical time? Why did I have such an aversion to entering into her deep sorrow and perplexity? Are these darker emotions antithetical to the life of faith?

Our Selfish Aversion to Pain and Grief

I have pondered these questions for a long time and have made several discoveries. First, I began to realize the depth of my selfishness and fear—and my acute need for more of God's grace. The Scriptures teach that selfishness permeates our hearts, but I had no idea how deep my own was until I got married. Many, if not most of us, get married with the illusion that we've finally found someone who will "love, adore, and care for me like no other." Our craving is not to serve but to be served. Like children scrambling for the biggest cookie on the plate, we cry, "Me first, me first!" My selfish desire to avoid dealing with my wife's pain made it easy for me to try to "fix" her. But Darlene's grief required more of me than I bargained for.

This same insensitivity and selfishness are recorded in Scripture. Only days before our Savior's death, his own disciples James and John approached Jesus with their mother. As the three of them bowed, their mom spoke up. "Jesus, will you do a favor for me?"

"What is your desire?" he inquired.

"Well, when you usher in your kingdom will you let one of my boys sit on your right and the other sit on your left?" In essence, they were jockeying for position.

That Jesus did not respond with disgust demonstrates the riches of his mercy. Instead, he said, "You have no idea what you are asking."

When the other disciples heard about this incident, however, "they were indignant"—perhaps because they hadn't thought of asking first. So Jesus reminded them, "Whoever wants to become great among you must be your servant and whoever wants to be first must be your slave—just as the Son of Man did not come to be served, but to serve, and to give his life as a ransom for many." His death would soon confirm the meaning of his words.

I find a certain relief in that story from Matthew 20. I am glad to see that even those who walked with Jesus for three years were capable of boneheaded selfishness. I am not alone! But I am even more comforted to see how forbearing Jesus is. To understand the heart of God is never to be surprised at the painful lengths he will go to free us from our enslavement to self-centeredness.

As God began to deal with me, he showed me three other reasons that made it easy for me to run from my wife's broken heart and deep confusion:

1. My triumphalistic gospel made no room for pain and suffering.
2. My formula-based theology required no faith or grace.
3. I had a deeply rooted fear of facing my *own* loss and grief.

Scratching Itching Ears

"Open your Bibles please to Romans 8:37. Today I am going to give you a life verse, a verse that I want you to make your own. Claim it for yourselves. Notice what Paul says: 'We are more than conquerors through him who loved us.' Mind you, *more* than conquerors, not just conquerors. Too many of you are living defeated lives. Where's your joy, your power? What kind of advertisement are you for the abundant life? Many Christians look a whole lot more like the conquered rather than the hyper-conquerors—(that's what the 'Greek' says)—we are called to be in Jesus. Are you the vanquished or the victor? . . ."

This kind of talk was characteristic of many Bible teachers in the late '60s and early '70s. Promoters of "triumphalism" were everywhere, offering promises, exhortations, and the key to living above the chaos of our fallen existence. They were easy to find and my heart naturally gravitated toward any teacher who could Christianize my well-rooted commitment to a life with no mess or pain.

Once, in college, when I was in the midst of a heated debate with a nonbeliever about the trustworthiness of the Bible, he sarcastically blurted out, "You Christians can make the Bible say anything you want it to say!" I've long since forgotten the outcome of the encounter, but I've never forgotten those words: "You Christians can make the Bible say *anything* you want it to say." As much as I disagreed with him then, I now realize his words are true—painfully and dangerously true.

The deceptive and destructive practice of distorting truth has been around ever since the beginning: "Did God really say, 'You must not eat from any tree in the garden'?" (Gen. 3:1). Satan was the first Scripture twister, and he set the precedent for our fallen human race. God had actually said, "You are free to eat from any tree in the garden; but you must not eat from the tree of the knowledge of good and evil, for when you eat of it you will surely die" (Gen. 2:16–17). But Satan, crafty as he is, seduced the woman by misrepresenting both God and his Word to her: "You will not surely die" (Gen. 3:4). He continues his work as the Father of Lies in every generation, sometimes overtly, more often covertly, as he appeals to our base instincts.

Or consider this example. Imagine a pastor saying, "Now read with me from your Bible, 'A thousand may fall at your side, ten thousand at your right hand, but it will not come near you. You will only observe with your eyes and see the punishment of the wicked. If you make the Most High your dwelling—even the LORD, who is my refuge—then no harm will befall you, no disaster will come near your tent' (Ps. 91:7–10). Do you see what God promises here? If you make him your dwelling place and your refuge, *nothing* bad will ever happen to you! Can you grasp the principle of faith in this text? Big faith, no disaster. Little faith, many disasters. Now, which do you want? A life of misery or a life of miracles? As God has said, 'You have not because you ask not.' Have you ever asked him for this kind of faith? It's a simple equation of faith. Just as Jesus said, 'Be it unto you according to your faith.' Many of you are sick, poor, depressed, and lonely for no other reason than a lack of faith. Screw up that faith button! Claim the promises."

Unfortunately, that is *exactly* how most bad teaching is generated. Verses are taken out of context and used to build a whole theology. More often than not, these distortions represent the depth of our commitment *not* to worship and serve God, but to do just the opposite. We want him to worship and serve us.

It is possible to hear good teaching but only believe a small part of it. We generally hear what we want to hear. The apostle Paul described a time when people "will not put up with sound doctrine. Instead, to suit their own desires, they will gather around them a great number of teachers to say what their itching ears want to hear. They will turn . . . aside to myths" (2 Tim. 4:3–4).

Perhaps no greater myth in our culture has caused more "ears to itch" than the one which insists, "I have a right to happiness and comfort." Before his death, Francis Schaeffer spoke of his concern that the two prevailing values among American Christians at the end of the twentieth century would become "personal peace and affluence." He seems to have been prophetic.

I gravitated toward the "victorious Christian life" teaching because it gave me a biblical way to control my world, manage God, and eliminate all mystery. Here are some of the legalistic "formulas" that Darlene and I believed to be biblical truths for the first few years of our married life together. This is the way the Christian life was "supposed to work." Do they sound familiar?

Consistent Daily Devotions + General Obedience = God's Blessings on Your Life

Longer Praying + More People Praying = Greater Predictability of Answered Prayer

Franklin, Tennessee. But I just talked with him today—he's dead? Who in the world would kill one of the most gentle men I've ever met?

As I drove up to the home, it looked like a scene from a movie: There were police cars, the fire department, neighbors standing around in disbelief, news crews were already beginning to arrive. A yellow plastic tape stretched around telephone poles in front of the home on which were printed those ominous words, POLICE CRIME SCENE. Then I looked in the garage, and there, on the ground in sur-real stillness, the sheet-covered body of my murdered friend.

Television crews, the police, the church, and the community were asking, "Where is God in all this?" I was as confused as anyone. As I watched the unfolding events—the search and capture of the one who did this horrible thing, the family trying to make plans, trying to answer their questions and make sense of the senseless—I felt so many emotions.

The funeral was actually the easiest part of the experience. I used Paul's words to troubled Christians in Thessalonica as my text, "Broth-ers, we do not want you to be ignorant about those who fall asleep; or to grieve like the rest of men, who have no hope" (1 Thess. 4:13). God is faithful and he faithfully met us. I'm not sure I have ever felt the Spirit's presence more profoundly than I did that day. But then, the day after the funeral, I received a letter that shook the foundation of my pastoral self-satisfaction. It proved to be a disturbing vehicle of God's grace.

A friend had written me to encourage and thank me for leading our church through a difficult week, but her parting words were used by God in a way she could not have anticipated: "Scotty, I think God has given you a special ability to detach yourself so that you can func-tion well and be strong for us." Like a laser-guided missile, those words penetrated my heart.

"Is this me, Lord? Is this who I really am? The pastor, the hus-band, the dad, the friend who can detach from any pain in such a way as to be helpful but not present in the loss? Dear God, surely this must be what Darlene has been lamenting so much of our married life."

All pastors expect to face the deaths of those in their congregations. I have officiated at many funerals. But now I was learning that there is a huge difference between walking a family through the process and being deeply involved with the grieving family yourself. Most deaths and funerals require about a week of intensive presence and love from a pastor. This death was demanding a lot more of me than a seven-day investment.

A couple of days later, Lou, Don's courageous wife, wanted a group of us to go with her to pray in the garage where Don had been murdered, to pray in his study, to go through the house, and ask our Father to begin the healing process. Still shaken by my friend's letter, I joined the small group of family and friends for what proved to be one of the most important times of prayer I have ever experienced.

We gathered in the garage and held hands in a circle on the very spot where Don had died. Praying for God's presence, crying out for wisdom and grace, our hearts became one. We went through other parts of the house until Lou asked a couple of us to go with her upstairs into the bedroom she shared with Don. Kneeling around the bed, Lou's heart broke and so did ours.

I sensed a nudging, an invitation from our Father not just to open my soul to Lou's pain but to go back further into my own. With our teary faces buried in Lou's bed as we prayed, I found myself beginning to feel the incredible pain of emptiness in my own home and heart after my mom's death. But this time I didn't run. Lingering there, I began to taste a freedom for which I had desperately longed but feared with my whole being. Tears started to come not simply from my eyes but from my frozen little-boy soul. There was no retreating from the ground gained by the Father that day.

Six months later came another call that proved to be the most painful phone message I have ever received. "Scotty, it's Rose Marie. Jack has died." Jack Miller—who had been my father in the gospel, friend, mentor, wise counsel, encourager, model of grace and boldness for twenty-one years—didn't make it through open-heart surgery. He and Rose Marie had gone to Spain to rest after a preaching and teaching

It is only those who are willing to wrestle with the mystery of hard providence who can speak with meaning about the astonishing reality of grace.

4. Grief gives us the opportunity to examine our priorities and relationships

We live too fast and too presumptuously. To know pain is to be given the chance to reevaluate those things we have allowed to claim our passions. I have never attended a dying man or woman who said to me, "I wish I had spent a lot more time at the office." According to our God, "The only thing that counts is faith expressing itself through love" (Gal. 5:6).

That which passes from this world to the next is people, not possessions. Some of us work with the illusion that the day is coming when we will be able to afford time with friends and family. If that day isn't today, that day will not come.

5. Grief has the power to transform us into a community of love

I have never met Nicholas Wolterstorff. After reading the book he wrote about the death of his son, *Lament for a Son*, I feel I know him well. Here is how he described his grief and grace:

> I shall look at the world through tears. Perhaps I will see things that dry eyed I could not see. If sympathy for the world's wounds is not enlarged by our anguish, if love for those around us is not expanded, if gratitude for what is good does not flame up, if insight is not deepened, if commitment to what is important is not strengthened, if aching for a new day is not intensified, if hope is weakened and faith diminished, if from the experience of death comes nothing good, then, death has won. Then death be proud.[3]

The bottom line is this: sometimes grief is the only way we really learn how to love.

chapter nine

[INFECTIOUS GRACE]

For the Sake of the Call

Nobody stood and applauded them
So they knew from the start
This road would not lead to fame
All they really knew for sure was Jesus had called to them
He said "Come follow me" and they came
With reckless abandon they came
Empty nets lying there at the water's edge
Told a story that few could believe and none could explain
How some crazy fishermen agreed to go where Jesus led
With no thought for what they would gain
For Jesus had called them by name and they answered

We will abandon it all for the sake of the call
No other reason at all but the sake of the call
Wholly devoted to live and to die
For the sake of the call

Drawn like the rivers are drawn to the sea
No turning back for the water cannot help but flow
Once we hear the Savior's call we'll follow wherever He leads
Because of the love He has shown
And because He has called us to go we will answer

We will abandon it all for the sake of the call
   No other reason at all but the sake of the call
   Wholly devoted to live and to die
   Not for the sake of a creed or a cause
   Not for a dream or a promise
   Simply because it is Jesus who calls
And if we believe we'll obey

Steven:

"Steven, my name is Larry Warren. Scotty tells me you have a heart for missions. I'd love to get together and chat."

To say that I had a "heart for missions" may have overstated the case, but it is true that ever since becoming a Christian I have had a hunch that God wants me involved, in some way, in world evangelization. More than once I have asked myself, "Should I be on the foreign missions field?" Meditating on the stories of godly people like Jim Elliot and Oswald Chambers has only served to stoke the missions embers that smolder inside me.

Larry and Scotty have been good friends since their days in North Carolina, where the two of them were involved together in a ministry as college students. After becoming a successful businessman, Larry received a call to use his gifts more directly in vocational ministry, especially in mobilizing Christians for ministry in Third World countries.

When I met him, Larry, his wife, Mary, and their two boys were living in South Africa in the racially divided region in Cape Town. "Have you ever thought of performing in South Africa?" Larry asked me.

Are you kidding? About all I knew of that strife-torn part of the world was the word *apartheid*. As Larry shared his passion and vision of God's grace bringing healing to this broken people, we agreed to pray and to see if God would, indeed, make such a trip possible for me and my band.

Sure enough, six dates came together as the last leg of my "Great Adventure Tour," allowing us to go to South Africa and to see firsthand both the dark, ravaging effects of sin and the beauty of what God is doing to redeem and to restore this magnificent part of his world.

Just days before we left, as our excitement began to peak, the news media started showing more and more images of violence in South Africa. Our wives, understandably, began to question the wisdom of our trip, and fear set in. In just three weeks, the first national nonracial election would be held, and no one could predict the outcome. It would be the first time that blacks and other nonwhites would be allowed to vote. Many whites were trying to book flights out of the country just as we were preparing to fly in! After more prayer with Larry, we decided to follow through with our plans, trust God, and (as we promised our wives) not do anything stupid!

The Scriptures teach that though we may make plans, God orders our steps. Our first few concerts went remarkably well. We performed twice in Johannesburg and twice in Durban. It surprised and humbled me to see how many people knew me and my music. As a band, we were overwhelmed with the welcome we received. But the well-ordered steps of our Father for this first trip became patently obvious at our two Cape Town concerts.

Cape Town is one of the most beautiful cities I have ever seen, with its incredible cliff-graced beaches, the majestic Table Mountain defining the horizon, its lush landscape, and magnificent architecture. But the most profound beauty was in the faces of about fifty children from the Xhosa tribe, whom Larry had arranged to bring to the concert from Kheyaleitsha, a black township about fifteen miles outside of Cape Town. Many of these children had never been to the city before.

After our concert, Larry and Laura Haas, the white European director of the Youth Center in Kheyaleitsha, brought several of these precious kids backstage to meet us, where, to our great joy, they performed for us! They danced and sang about Jesus with so much sincerity and passion—our hearts were captured! With childlike innocence, they begged us to come and visit their township the next morning.

Tension time, decision time! I suddenly remembered one of my last, preboarding conversations with Mary Beth. "Oh, no, honey. You don't need to worry. We won't be going anywhere near the black townships. We're walking by faith, but we're not going to unnecessarily endanger ourselves. Larry is going to take good care of us." What to do!

In my work with Chuck Colson and Prison Fellowship, I have come to understand a little of what Mother Teresa used to refer to as "looking for Jesus in disguise." I have discovered the presence of Jesus in some of the most oppressive and degrading circumstances, including maximum security prisons and death row itself. I want to be where Jesus would be—and where he is. To look into the eyes of these children was to experience a glimmer of the arresting gaze of our Lord. After covering every conceivable base, we decided to go to Kheyaleitsha with Larry and Laura the next morning.

Nothing could have prepared us for what we experienced. How is it possible to squeeze a million people onto a five-by-ten-mile rectangle of flat sand? Row after row after row of what appeared to be cardboard, tin, and baling-wire shacks. If apartheid had only been a political word before this morning, it now became an ugly reality. How can human dignity be maintained in such despicable circumstances? The contrast between the squalor of Kheyaleitsha and the luxuries of Cape Town made it seem as though they were fifteen centuries apart rather than fifteen miles. It would be like driving from the well-heeled districts of San Francisco to the slums of Port-au-Prince, Haiti, in fifteen minutes.

As we approached the Youth Center, we were greeted by hundreds of smiling and appreciative Xhosas. You would have thought that we were royalty—or Nelson Mandela himself, who is a member of the Xhosas tribe. After performing an impromptu concert to the delight of an ever-swelling crowd, it was God's turn to perform for us through this amazing group of believers. I have had the privilege of traveling to many parts of the world and observing the hand and heart of God in action in incredible ways, but nothing has made a greater impression than seeing God's grace manifest in the lives of these Christians.

They danced, sang, and worshiped God with simplicity and joy in the midst of the most horrid living conditions I have never seen. It made me think of the Christians in Macedonia whom Paul described as being full of "rich generosity" and "overflowing joy" even though they lived in "extreme poverty" and were under "severe trial" (2 Cor. 8:1).

The image of God expanded in my soul that day. These precious believers helped me realize that our Lord is much bigger and more powerful than I had thought. Awe filled my soul.

After many hugs, we boarded our vehicle to leave, but a part of me is still there in the Kheyaleitsha slums with some of the richest Christians I will ever hope to meet. A mighty and merciful act of God is going on among them, a small foretaste of the new heaven and the new earth. God is redeeming the worst of sin and death, and a garden is springing up in the desert. This was no mere Kodak Moment in the scrapbook of the travels of Steven Curtis Chapman. I knew that day I would be here again, next time with my family.

Full-Time Missionaries?

"Honey, are you ready to sell the farm and move? I really believe that a part of our future is in helping develop that Youth Center in Kheyaleitsha, and maybe this is the very call we have mused about through the years."

Mary Beth and I have had a running conversation for a long time about getting rid of everything and making a drastic lifestyle change. Sometimes, that impulse comes in the middle of the mounting stress of making a living as a musician; sometimes it comes in those quiet moments of pondering the values of heaven. This time those two themes seemed to come together with equal force.

One evening, Scotty and I sat in the Nashville Arena on the evening of the Dove Awards ceremony. Being a presenter, nominee, and performer, I should have been both excited and humbled. In reality, I was confused and uncertain. "Can we go for a walk, buddy?" I said.

As Scotty and I strolled around the massive arena, now filling up with thousands of people coming to the biggest event of Gospel Music Association Week, I asked Scotty, "Do you think this season of my life is over? Is it time for me to make the big change? I'm not sure that big arenas, stressful tours, and Dove Awards are what it's all about."

My restlessness continued until Mary Beth and I finally decided to pack our kids onto a big jet bound for South Africa. All five of us were packed for what I had a hunch would be our final destination. I really expected "the call" to come at some point on our trip. "Lord, when is the bolt of lightning going to hit us? As we lift off the runway?

When we land in South Africa? Will all five of us hold hands in a circle right beside the Kheyaleitsha Youth Center and agree to send for our belongings? Maybe I should have had enough faith just to buy us one-way tickets!"

While I romanticized my "missions moment," my son Caleb spilled his second drink, getting sticky apple juice all over himself at the beginning of our seventeen-hour flight! Suddenly the dream of my family being the next little missionary family "on the field" got a dose of reality. We didn't leave our sinful hearts in Williamson County. As the flight continued it appeared less and less likely that this would be the supernatural moment I had anticipated. I began to feel the same stress and pressures that I felt on my big tours. "Lord, this isn't the way it's supposed to be."

It seems that God's Spirit stirs my soul in the midst of the confusing moments of life. I took out a piece of paper and a pen and tried to give expression to the mounting sense of restlessness within. I began to journal my feelings and a song emerged out of the chaos called "Be Still and Know":

Be still and know that He is God
Be still and know that He is holy
Be still, O restless soul of mine
Bow before the Prince of peace
Let the noise and clamor cease
Be still

Be still and know that He is God
Be still and know that He is faithful
Consider all that he has done
Stand in awe and be amazed
And know that He will never change
Be still

Be still and know that he is God
Be still and know he is our Father
Come rest your head upon his breast

Listen to the rhythm of his unfailing heart of love
Beating for His little ones
Calling each of us to come
Be still

This song helped me, once again, to realize that God is God—and I am not. He is in control. He doesn't need me to do anything; he simply delights in me as his son. He is more pleased when I sit before him in silence than when I put my activist hat on and try to save the world. I needed to give up the idol of a perfect little missionary family even before we landed in South Africa.

Well, that seventeen-hour flight finally came to an end, and after deboarding, we began to see the wonders of God's creation in the animal world of Africa and his re-creation in Kheyaleitsha, both of which bring him great glory.

When asked by one of the South Africans soon after setting foot on their native soil, "Steven, what message do you bring to our people?" I was speechless. I hadn't thought of bringing a "word." I reflected a few minutes and then shared the story of the song I wrote on the flight on the way down. "Brothers, I come to be still and to listen to what God is saying and to see what he is already doing among you. This is a season for me to be quiet before him and to enjoy participating in the expansion of his kingdom everywhere in his world and to acknowledge that he is the King, not me. My restless heart needs to rest in him and not in my plans to do his work. And I long for this same rest and peace to come to your country through the healing grace and power of the gospel."

Larry planned our itinerary, and we met many incredible new friends in the Lord. But one of the greatest surprises occurred as we were told that proceeds from my benefit concerts would go to "Music for Missions"—a group of South African Christian young people who were raising money to come to America to minister to us in light of the great needs that they perceive *we* have in our homeland! What an awesome lesson in humility and in working together for the expansion of the kingdom of God. Our God is so big and so good. Their riches can supply our needs, and our riches can meet their needs. Surely God is praised when we serve one another.

Needless to say, we returned to "the farm" in Franklin, Tennessee. God did not call us to South Africa, but he did call us to himself in a fresh and profound way—and that is the most important calling of all. We have committed to keep exposing ourselves to the work of the kingdom around the world. We have promised to keep our hearts and resources malleable in the hands of the Great Potter who may, indeed, call us in a different career direction in the future. It is just too easy to get sucked back into our ingrown lifestyle, forgetting that we are a part of God's plan for all of history and for all of the nations of the world.

Short-term missions trips will continue to be a part of our lives, and we are thrilled to deepen our commitment to the Youth Center in Kheyaleitsha. Our daughter, Emily, may well end up with a calling to cross-cultural missions. Nothing would thrill us more. As for now, my music allows me to minister in ways that I hadn't appreciated before.

Still, I am no less restless. But I have a sneaky hunch that it is a redemptive restlessness. I know that I am not home yet and my yearning for my final home grows more intense. But life now is not about me, it's about the spread of the gospel of God's grace and the expansion of his kingdom, in Franklin, Kheyaleitsha, and in every square inch of the universe. God's grace will continue to disrupt my little paradigms until Jesus returns. I rest in that truth even as I purpose to stay still and know that God is God.

Scotty:

Grace Multiplied in Death

"He is no fool who will give what he cannot keep to gain what he cannot lose." Those passionate words, spoken by Jim Elliot, a young missionary from Wheaton College, took on a whole new meaning as we gathered in the little country cemetery to commit Jack Miller's body to the earth. I dreaded this moment, this final good-bye.

The night before, the memorial service had taken me through the gamut of emotions—from deep sadness to great joy when I witnessed how much of God's grace can be crammed into sixty-five brief years of life.

As the worship center quickly filled with nearly two thousand friends, colleagues, and family members, hugs and glad greetings abounded. We gathered to worship our wonderful merciful Savior and to reflect on one life well lived. Joy and gratitude prevailed as family members recounted story after story of the overflow of Christ's love through a dad and granddad.

Perhaps the loudest testimony to the power of the gospel came from two pastors who shared their hearts. Bob, a former heroin addict, who Jack picked up as a hitchhiker, took home, and led to Christ, spoke first: "Jack used to tell us, 'Throw away your self-protection and be a fool for Christ.' We have never known a less foolish man."

The other pastor, Angelo, had been a junkie who plied his trade on innocent young people in Philadelphia. Jack met him and mounted a "love offensive" until one day Angelo capitulated to the mercy and grace of God. In his impassioned sermon he bid us to "believe the gospel and rely more fully on the great love of God lavished on ourselves and extended to the nations of the world." Even more remarkable is the fact that these men—both former drug addicts—are married to Jack's daughters!

With hearts and hands raised to heaven, we celebrated Jesus' triumph over sin and death as we sang, "Joy to the world! The Lord is come . . . He rules the world with truth and grace. . . ." "No condemnation now I dread; Jesus, and all in Him, is mine! Alive in Him, my living Head and clothed in righteousness divine, bold I approach th' eternal throne. . . ." "Arise, my soul arise, shake off thy guilty fears: The bleeding sacrifice in my behalf appears: Before the Throne my Surety stands . . . My name is written on his hands. . . . With confidence I now draw nigh, and 'Father, Abba, Father!' cry." My great loss seemed to be swallowed up and redefined in the presence of so much joy and grace.

A Little Seed—A Big Harvest

Walking the short distance to the grave, time seemed to slow down. Images of some of God's other "peculiar" people came to mind, images of lives infected with the joy, simplicity, and the purity of devotion to Jesus. Their common denominator was that, like Jack, they were all dedicated to missionary work overseas.

I thought of Jim Elliot and his four friends, who were speared to death by a group of Auca Indians as they sought to share the gospel of God's grace with this small tribe of sixty natives who had never before heard the name Jesus. As college students, they gathered faithfully at 6:30 each morning to pray. They longed for God to call forth more men and women from the Wheaton student body who would find their lives by losing themselves in taking the gospel to the nations of the world. Jim Elliot's wife lived to see the fruit of this sacrifice of love as the tribesman who killed her husband became a Christian and was baptized before her very eyes.

Yet another remarkable life came to mind. For fifty-five consecutive years Amy Carmichael, born into a wealthy family in Northern Ireland, lived among the poorest of the poor in South India for the purpose of rescuing girls who had been dedicated to a life of ritual prostitution in Hindu temples. In the midst of long days of endless needs, Amy managed to write thirty-five books in her spare time. After Amy's death at the age of eighty-one, a close friend commented, "Her life was the most fragrant, the most joyfully sacrificial, that I ever knew."

The same "sacrificial joy" echoed in Jack's own great laugh. I miss hearing that laugh as much as I have ever missed anything. "Father, what do I know of this kind of joy, which mocks the grave and is not tricked by the so-called toys, trinkets, and riches of this world?" I asked myself as we gathered at Jack's headstone to hear the reading of the Scriptures.

Through the joyful and selfless witness of Jim Elliot and Amy Carmichael, thousands of people have been deeply encouraged to risk everything to carry the gospel among the unreached people groups of the world. Such is the infectious impact of a single life freed by the grace of God and enflamed with a vision of heaven crowded with joyful men and women of every race, tribe, and tongue.

As the service continued, I could not help but think about the similarities between Jim Elliot, Amy Carmichael, and Jack—their influence was contagious. Though Jack had not died as a martyr, he lived as one. He died to self every day in light of one consuming passion: to see the glory and grace of Jesus proclaimed among the nations of the world. Like a grace magnet, he attracted those whose polarity was heaven. It astonished and encouraged me to look around that little cemetery and see several of my friends and seminary buddies who were led to take huge risks of faith and love because of this one little grace-driven life.

There stood Dan Herron, a seminary classmate, who for the last several years had been serving in the rural mountains of Uganda. There was Bill Scott, a friend from college days who flew in from Kenya where he ministered the gospel before moving to Berlin, Germany. There was Hunter Dockery, a Bible study friend from North Carolina who was now a church planter in Ireland. There was Bob Heppe, a friend, whom I met soon after his conversion, now the leader of a church-planting effort in London among the people of Asia. In all, I counted seven of these men—all serving Christ among the nations of the world because of Jack's joy in the gospel and excitement about the world harvest!

Among the invited guests was Dr. Wolfgang Wegert, the pastor of a church in Hamburg, Germany. At the graveside service, he said, "Brothers and sisters, I bring you greetings even as I share in your sadness. Just two months ago our Lord used Dr. Miller to open a door to the grace of the gospel in our church. Little did any of us realize that this would be his last preaching mission. His joy and love were infectious. Perhaps, the effect of his one brief visit will be felt throughout Germany for years to come."

Jack used to tell us, "There is no limit to what God can do through the man or woman who doesn't care who gets the credit." He proved those words were no mere maxim. I shook my head in glad disbelief when Wolfgang said, "This anonymous little man has affected the nations of the world."

Who would have thought that a cemetery would become a place for the refueling of a whole missionary movement? I found myself saying, "What about you, Scotty? How are you planning on investing the rest of your life? Has pastoring a big church made you complacent? Are you already thinking about retirement?"

Before Jack's death, I had promised him I would make a follow-up trip to Hamburg, since I couldn't accompany him on the first mission there. So, after the funeral, Wolfgang and I talked briefly about my desire to bring a team to his church, but my immediate interest lay in finding out how he and Jack had met in the first place. He told me the story.

"Joni Eareckson Tada spoke in our church," said Wolfgang, "about God's goodness in the midst of her suffering. This was during a time when I had many questions about God's sovereignty and his grace. I asked her if she knew anyone who could be of help to me in these matters. She said, 'I know a little man in Philadelphia, Pennsylvania, who knows as much about God's grace as anyone I have met. Perhaps he can help you.'"

Jack and Wolfgang had met only once, but the bond of love between them was such that Wolfgang felt compelled to fly with his wife all the way from Germany to attend Jack's funeral.

As the dirt filled the grave and we began to leave, the words of Jesus came to mind, "Unless a kernel of wheat falls to the ground and dies, it remains only a single seed. But if it dies, it produces many seeds. The man who loves his life will lose it, while the man who hates his life in this world will keep it for eternal life. Whoever serves me must follow me; and where I am, my servant also will be. My Father will honor the one who serves me" (John 12:24–26).

Walking back to the car with Darlene, I found myself praying, "Lord, help me not simply idolize the Jim Elliots, Amy Carmichaels, and Jack Millers of this world. I am tempted to put them in a whole different category of humanity than myself, as though you could never make of me such a man. What is keeping me from abandoning myself to your purposes for history and my life? Deal with me, Lord."

Surprised by Grace

Six months after standing in that cemetery, I stood in the Hamburg airport with six good friends from our church family. We were there to continue the work started by Jack in Pastor Wolfgang Wegert's church. "Welcome, welcome, friends." Big German bear hugs enveloped us as Wolfgang and some of his staff picked us up at the airport. As we drove from the airport, Wolfgang shared his heart with us: "We have been praying for your time here. So many of our people are just beginning to come alive to the grace of God. Our tradition and culture makes a 'works' form of Christianity very attractive and safe for us. We are a hardworking people. We have all kinds of questions since Jack's visit."

"Great," I said, "Jack gets you stirred up and then takes off for heaven, leaving me to clean up his mess!" We laughed.

We arrived at the church that would be home for our week in Hamburg, a beautiful port city on the northern border of Germany. After settling in and sharing our first delicious German meal, we went over the schedule for the week. "Scotty and team members," said Wolfgang, "it is wonderful to have you here for this week of studying the theme of the riches of God's grace. Now, tomorrow morning we will need to leave about eight o'clock to drive to downtown Hamburg where, Scotty, you will preach and your music team will perform."

Wolfgang could hardly get those words out of his mouth before we looked at one another with shock and great surprise. "We're going to do what?" This trip to the inner city for open-air ministry had not been written into *our* itinerary. We had planned on a nice safe Bible conference in which the music team would lead worship and I would teach and preach on the wonders of God's grace.

God has a remarkable way of arranging circumstances so as to drive us to our knees and to himself! I had *never* "street preached" by myself in English, much less through a German translator! This felt a lot more intimidating than being in the Gypsy camps of southern

Spain, where Jack did all the preaching and I stood behind him as a prayer warrior! Our team didn't do a lot of sleeping that night, but we did do a lot of praying and practicing some music that could be performed in a busy marketplace. "Father, thank you for your gracious sense of humor! We surrender ourselves to your love for the peoples of the world and your love for us. Take our fears, our love of approval, our insecurities and free us."

Next day, we set up in the center of the busiest square in Hamburg. Wolfgang gathered us together for a final word of encouragement. "By the way, if people start heckling you or try to interrupt your music and preaching, don't worry, we're close by." Some encouragement! We offered a final prayer and a strange sense of peace and joy came over us. Once again, Jim Elliot's words came to mind. "He is no fool who gives what he cannot keep to gain what he cannot lose." "Lord," we prayed, "help us freely and fearlessly give those who pass by a taste of the grace you have lavished upon us. Free us from the paralyzing power of loving the approval of others."

As we began to play our music, much to our surprise, a crowd gathered, no doubt intrigued by this odd bunch of American minstrels. When it came time to preach, my nervousness gave way to peace. "Men and women of Hamburg," I started, "we are here to proclaim to you the Good News of God's great love freely offered to any who will receive it." My translator spoke with passion and tenderness for his fellow countrymen.

We continued to sing and preach for a couple of hours. The longer we were there the greater our joy became. We invited one and all to come and join us for the series of meetings at Wolfgang's church. I have absolutely no idea if anyone from that morning outreach came, but I do know that God began a great work in each of *our* hearts. For a whole morning we shared the rich blessing and freedom of self-forgetfulness. "Is this what being a fool for Christ feels like?" one of our team asked. "If so, may God make me an even bigger fool."

As we were packing up our equipment and looking forward to a big lunch of schnitzel and sauerkraut, someone in the crowd came up to me and said, "Did you notice the statue you set up in front of? Do you know who this man is? Gotthold Ephraim Lessing, the father of modern higher criticism of the Bible. He is honored as the scholar who rescued our German society, and then the whole Western world, from a 'superstitious childlike belief in the Bible.' I thought it was pretty ironic that you were sharing the gospel in his shadow!" That proved to be just another of God's little gifts to us!

It's a Small, Small World

The rest of the week contained one surprise after another. *"Como sey yamo? Me yamo es Señor Smith!"* Who would have thought that a German church would have a group of Spanish members in it? Steve Green had flown over to join us for an outreach concert, and a national cheer went up from an enthusiastic crowd when he began to sing in Spanish!

For just a moment I experienced a taste of what it is going to be like when Jesus comes back and all of his bride gathers before him. The apostle John describes his vision of that incredible day this way:

I looked and there before me was a great multitude that no one could count, from every nation, tribe, people and language, standing before the throne and in front of the Lamb. They were wearing white robes and were holding palm branches in their hands. And they cried out in a loud voice: "Salvation belongs to our God, who sits on the throne, and to the Lamb." (Rev. 7:9–10)

Our world got even smaller as the week went on. Wolfgang shared his longing to take the gospel of God's grace deeper into the massive country of India. With amusement and delight, we watched some videos of this huge German pastor preaching—with his words dubbed into an Indian dialect. His burden for India reminded me of one of my favorite adventures with Jack. "Wolfgang," I said, "a group of us were on a prayer walk through Southhall, an area in south London that is largely populated by transplanted Indians. As we walked and prayed through the business district, Jack noticed a Hindu temple. 'Let me see if I can get permission for us to have a tour,' he said. He went inside and in a few moments returned with a gracious lady who seemed more than glad to share her faith and place of worship with us.

"Well, she led us into a dimly lit room, lined with several altars along the walls where worshipers offered sacrifices and prayers to a variety of deities. I found myself inwardly mocking what appeared to be large plastic female dolls and other odd idols which were representations of various gods.

"But then I watched as Jack showed great respect and love for our hostess. As we finished the tour he asked permission to share his faith with her, which she was most willing for him to do. So for the next ten minutes, right in the middle of a Hindu temple, Jack tenderly and boldly spoke of the glory and grace of the one true living God and his Son, Jesus. As we were leaving, he invited this kind woman to join us and several other Indians as our guests for lunch the next day. Much to my surprise, she actually came, and we had a delightful time reflecting on the knowledge of God. Jack's belief in the welcoming heart of God made him so willing to share with anyone, anywhere, anytime. His vision of a filled-up heaven compelled him to love with abandon!"

A common quest to share the love of God bound us together there in Hamburg. Wolfgang said, "Scotty, the more I learn about God's sovereign grace, the more I long to see Germany come alive again to the faith we knew during Martin Luther's day. We have lost so much of our spiritual heritage. I am praying that we will fall in love with him again so we can be a light to the nations. What else is worth living for?"

Our week in Hamburg passed all too fast. We spent hours with our new friends discussing what the Scriptures say about the glorious implications of God's grace. We found our German brothers and sisters to be just like the rest of us. We all struggle with believing that God really loves as much as he says he does. Unbelief is probably the core sin in each of our hearts.

I went away from that trip pondering the common denominator in the lives of Jim Elliot, Amy Carmichael, and Jack Miller, and others like them who, with joy, give themselves to world evangelization. What makes the difference? While others are content to have a little Christian house and family in the "burbs," these women and men are bored silly and senseless with such a small dream and limited horizon.

What explains the holy restlessness that drives them to invest themselves in eternity rather than wasting away in an endless pursuit of "personal peace and affluence"? Is it their extraordinary gifts, talents, and skills as visionaries and organizers? Could it be their zealous commitment to "get the job done," living with a disciplined commitment to dutifully fulfill the Great Commission? Maybe its their missiological training, biblical convictions, and strategies for reaching the unreached people of the world.

While gifts, zeal, and training are present, what separates these selfless women and men from the rest of us is their extraordinary awareness of the love of Christ. Each of them, in their own way, shows what the apostle Paul meant by these words, "If we are out of our mind, it is for the sake of God; if we are in our right mind, it is for you. For Christ's love compels us, because we are convinced that one died for all, and therefore all died. And he died for all, that those who live should no longer live for themselves but for him who died for them and was raised again" (2 Cor. 5:13–15). The compelling love of Christ experienced in the gospel of God's grace is the common denominator in all of these lives.

What About Us?

It's been three years since we buried Jack. My heart is more redemptively restless than ever as I ponder my remaining years in this world. God continues to bring sovereign surprises into my life, which all point toward a greater involvement in his international grace harvest.

This past year our church generously gave me a sabbatical, which my wife and I spent at Covenant Seminary in St. Louis. While there I joined a "covenant group," a gathering of ten to twelve students who gather on a weekly basis with a member of the faculty for the purpose of prayer and mutual support. For the first time in my life I knew what it felt like to be a minority.

"Welcome, everyone. I'm Hans Bayer from southern Germany, and I teach New Testament here at Covenant. Why don't we take a minute to introduce ourselves." "My name is Olga, and I am from Russia." "I'm Kor from the Netherlands." "I'm Tom, and my family is en route to southern England." "My home is in South Africa, and my name is Alice." "We're Jon and Julie from Holland." "My name is Sandra, and I live in Berlin." "I'm Simon from Kampala, Uganda." "We're Rene and Loni from the Philippines." "My name is Scotty, and I'm from Franklin, Tennessee." For some reason my introduction didn't have quite the same snap to it!

As the year progressed my connection with the international body of Christ intensified. These are my brothers and sisters, my family—not cultural oddities or strangers. To pray with Olga that her parents might have enough heating oil to last through the winter; to grieve with Simon over the death of his father in Kampala and to weep with him one week later when his first child died in her mother's womb; to pray for Hans as he went into Kiev to teach New Testament Introduction to hungry young converts; to pray with Sandra for her unconverted family back in Germany; to support Tom as he moved his wife and five children to English L'Abri; to marvel at Rene and Loni as they prepare to take the gospel to south Malaysia in a Muslim population where two of their friends have already suffered a martyr's death—need I say more?

John Stott summarizes the centrality of our call to missions:

> Our mandate for world evangelization is the whole Bible. It is to be found in the creation of God (because of which all human beings are responsible to him), in the character of God (as outgoing, loving, compassionate, not willing that any should perish, desiring that all should come to repentance), in the promises of God (that all nations will be blessed through Abraham's seed and will become the Messiah's inheritance), in the Christ of God (now exalted with universal authority, to receive universal

acclaim), in the Spirit of God (who convicts of sin, witnesses to Christ, and impels the church to evangelize) and in the church of God (which is a multinational, missionary community, under orders to evangelize until Christ returns).[1]

How can this calling become our heart's delight as opposed to being a burden on our guilty consciences? Like many of you, I have suffered through Missions Conferences and "Missions Moments" in various worship services from which I went away feeling bad about my spirituality because I was not packing my bags to go overseas and "do missions." Too often the Great Commission was presented to me as a "job to get done" with guilt-producing jabs such as, "If you won't go, who will?" But that is *not* what God wants us to feel.

We serve a God who, in the joy of his own passion, challenges us, like Abraham, to count the stars, to count the grains of sand on the shores, even to count the dust . . . (Genesis 15). These images are meant to convey to us how big God's family will be in the new heavens and the new earth. Impossible? That is just the point! Our Father has determined to fill up heaven with men and women from *every* race, tribe, and tongue—from *every* period in history. This is *his* promise, this is *his* covenant, this is *his* doing!

The whole Bible, from Genesis to Revelation, is a record of the unfolding of God's commitment to redeem for himself a people to love with great delight, forever. Salvation is of the Lord. God invites us to be astonished, to be left speechless, not at "how much *we* have to accomplish before Jesus returns," rather to be in awe of how much *he* is accomplishing before sending Jesus back—to be staggered at the enormity of his mercy—to marvel at such a demonstration of grace and compassion—to be alive to the outpouring of his redeeming love for the nations of the world. We must see in the cross of Christ not simply the means by which all of this is *possible* but the *guarantee* that it will be realized in full.

Ours is the privilege of entering into the secured harvest. The visions recorded for us in the book of Revelation of the multinational, transgenerational people of God gathered in worship around the throne of grace are meant to deeply encourage us about the outcome of the history of the world (Rev. 4, 5, 7). These visions are not possibilities or even probabilities. They are the actualities of our God who does not lie! These things *will* be.

Missions is not about what we *have* to do but what we *get* to do. It has pleased our Father to use us, even us, to accomplish matters settled before the creation of the world. Astonishing! Instead of merely watching Brady Bunch reruns and reunion movies, we get to invest our passion, hearts, gifts, and days in that which really matters, the filling up of heaven and the redeeming of our culture. What a privilege!

chapter ten

[LIVING IN LIGHT OF HEAVEN]

Heaven in the Real World

I saw it again today in the face of a little child
Looking through the eyes of fear and uncertainty
It echoed in a cry for freedom across the street and across
the miles
Cries from the heart to find the missing part

Where is the hope, where is the peace?
That will make this life complete
For every man, woman, boy and girl
Looking for heaven in the real world

To stand in the pouring rain and believe the sun will
shine again
To know that the grave is not the end
To feel the embrace of grace and cross the line where
real life begins
And know in your heart you've found the missing
part

There is a hope, there is a peace
That will make this life complete
For every man, woman, boy and girl
Looking for heaven in the real world
Heaven in the real world

It happened one night with a tiny baby's birth
God heard creation crying and He sent heaven to earth

He is the hope, He is the peace
That will make this life complete
For every man, woman, boy and girl
Looking for heaven in the real world
He is the hope, He is the peace
That will make this life complete
For every man, woman, boy and girl
Looking for heaven in the real world
Heaven has come to the real world
Heaven has come, come to the real world
He is the hope, He is the peace
Jesus is heaven, heaven in the real world

Steven:

The lilting sound of a harp wafts through the atmosphere. Cherublike creatures float peacefully by with rosy cheeks, curly blond hair, and dimpled smiles. In the distance, a gathering of white-robed adults, a hundred or more, walk on what appears to be a cloudlike floor in a brilliant haziness. Everyone moves slowly and deliberately with an obvious sense of peace and calm.

Most of the men have neatly cropped beards and the women all look pretty much alike—attractive, thirty-three-year-old, white American females with medium-length brunette hair and milky complexions. Suddenly, the music grows louder, this time accompanied by what sounds like a whole orchestra with a huge brass section.

A bright light to my left swells and gets more intense, as though someone were turning up a rheostat. Walking through the scene are what look like Bible characters as I have always envisioned them. I wonder if that one who looks so much like Charlton Heston is Moses! Those guys must be the apostles; I recognize them from the pictures on the wall of our church fellowship hall.

The music crescendos. Someone else is walking behind the apostles. I think—maybe, just maybe, yes!—it is! It's Jesus! I'd recognize him anywhere. He looks just like my Sunday school handouts, with a lamb on his shoulders and that beautiful shiny brunette hair. Look at him as he walks among the adoring crowd, so kind, so approachable.

What is that low rumbling noise? It sounds like thunder, but it's not threatening. That's the voice of God. I can't quite make out what he's saying, but all the people listen attentively and fall on their faces in adoration. Where did all of those big-winged, singing angels suddenly come from? They must be the famous heavenly host I've read about in the Bible. They sing louder and louder! Just as I figured, it's the "Hallelujah Chorus"! Everybody is joining in! Wow, I can't wait to get here—I think.

Will the Real Heaven Please Stand Up

Of course, considering the alternative, any of us will be glad to go to heaven—no matter *what* it's like. But how we conceive of heaven

195

matters greatly. The preceding paragraphs incorporated all those images of heaven we pick up as children from our culture, Sunday school, our own imaginations, and, yes, even from bathroom tissue commercials. It's scary to realize where many of us get our picture of eternity!

The first time I really got excited about heaven—our eternal home—was ten years ago when I worked at Lorenz Music with my buddy Tony Ellenberg. Still green in the world of music, I seized every opportunity to learn from my mentors in contemporary Christian music. Dallas Holm, one of my all-time favorite people and artists, came to Two Rivers Baptist Church, and during the course of his concert, he told this story: "My son asked my wife one night recently, 'Mommy, will there be bears in heaven?'

"She responded, 'Well, sweetheart, God made bears to live in his first garden, I suppose there will be bears in heaven. Why not?'

"'Mommy, will there be snakes in heaven. I like snakes, and what about lions?'

"'Darling, I know the Bible talks about lions eating straw again. Maybe you will get to pet one then, just like it were a big old sweet doggie.'

"So far so good, but then he asked, 'What about dinosaurs? Will there be dinosaurs in heaven?'

"My wife spontaneously replied, 'Honey, why don't you go ask your dad that one!'"

We all howled, but then Dallas said, "Charge me with heresy, but I've got a feeling we will be able to fly in heaven!" The concert resumed, but for the next two days I could not wipe a big grin off of my face as I thought about the possibility of flying. It was one of my childhood dreams. I have always wanted to get on top of a high mountain and just take off into the sky. No, it's not a subtle death wish, just an awesome longing to be that free and mobile to move about God's incredible universe. I've yet to find a chapter and verse for flying, but at least I have been rescued from lesser thoughts of what God tells us "no eye has seen, no ear has heard, nor has it even entered into the mind of man the things that he has prepared for those who love him." I move that we all give up our feeble ideas of heaven!

A Few Years and a Little Better Theology Later

A few years later I decided to write a song or two about heaven. This impulse led to what became my "Heaven in the Real World" record and tour. In preparation for this project, Scotty and I had some great discussions about our eternal abode and how God wants us to spend more time pondering our destiny and destination.

He told me about Richard Baxter, an English pastor of the sixteenth century, who wrote a classic book on heaven while imprisoned for his faith, entitled *The Saints' Everlasting Rest*. Baxter strongly recommended that Christians meditate upon heaven for at least thirty minutes a day. He believed it was the most powerful way to get the grace of God deep into the hearts of Christians—and to get Christians into the world as God's representatives.

Since heaven is the fullest and final expression of God's love and grace operating in the world, then it stands to reason that we should be influenced *now* by the way things will be *then*. Heaven, as it really is, should have a dramatic effect on how we live as Christians in this world. The old adage about being "so heavenly minded you are of no earthly good" is simply not true. The problem is not preoccupation with heaven but preoccupation with wrong notions about heaven. Little wonder that many of us are not in a hurry to leave our comfortable little worlds for some of the trite and sappy images we've been given. Materialistically we sing about "building our mansions next door to Jesus" while we order our "heavenly hams." Help!

Where Is Heaven, Anyway?

Scotty had been teaching through the book of Revelation and had all kinds of passion and fresh convictions about time and eternity. "Finally, Steven, I understand a little bit more of what the apostle Paul talked about when he said, 'No eye has seen, no ear has heard, no mind has conceived what God has prepared for those who love him'

(1 Cor. 2:9). Heaven is so much more than we ever longed for or even dared to desire."

There is a lot we cannot say for sure about heaven, but this we can affirm: "You will fill me with joy in your presence, with eternal pleasures at your right hand" (Ps. 16:11). Our heavenly Father intends to overload our circuits with joy! Heaven is going to be an eternal state of absolute blessedness and satisfaction primarily because of our perfected relationship with God our Father. Finally, we will be free to glorify God and to *enjoy* him forever! Such thoughts are unfathomable to our finite minds, but the Scriptures *shout* the good news: Heaven is going to be a realm of unsurpassed joy, unfading glory, undiminished bliss, unlimited delights, and unending pleasures!

John Stott offers this wisdom:

> There is no need for us to speculate about the precise nature of heaven. We are assured on the authority of Jesus Christ that it is the house and home of his Father and ours (there are twenty-two references to the Father in John 14), that this home is a prepared place containing many rooms or resting places, and that he himself will be there. What more do we need to know? To be certain that where he is, there we shall be also should be enough to satisfy our curiosity and allay our fears.[1]

A Heavenly Garden

But what *can* we safely deduce from Scripture about heaven without falling into wild speculation? Scotty helped me realize that any discussion about heaven should take us to the first book in the Bible, to the first few chapters of Genesis. The Garden of Eden is one of the best glimpses God gives us of the way life will be in eternity. The first two chapters of Genesis describe the way God designed his people and his creation to exist in relationship with one another.

God created a magnificent universe to reflect his glory and said, "It is good." A world of rivers, animals, all the lushness of a garden, sun, moon, and stars, oceans full of life, the cycle of day and night— what an amazing design! And then, to top it off, he created man, made in his own image—male and female, Adam and Eve. He gave them the privilege of living in rich relationship with himself and the responsibility of caring for his creation. They were charged to "be fruitful and increase in number; fill the earth and subdue it" (Gen. 1:28).

I got imagination overload just trying to envision how awesome life must have been before the Fall. Everything existed in perfect relationship: Adam and Eve enjoyed a perfect relationship with God, knowing, loving, and serving him. Adam and Eve's marriage must have been incredible, nakedness with absolutely no shame or selfishness! Living peacefully with animals of every variety in an unspoiled environment—no smog, no thin ozone layer, no carcinogens—even work was a complete joy and satisfaction. It seems too good to be true!

It's important to see that life in the Garden wasn't exactly what we think of in terms of "religious activity" all the time. Every day did not begin and end with a Bible study and prayer meeting. Adam and Eve lived out their relationship with God in every area of their lives. Life didn't consist of one big spiritual meeting. They met with him in "the cool of the day" for fellowship and communion, but God created every sphere of life to be a testimony to his goodness and majesty.

Nor was there a distinction between sacred and secular before Adam and Eve rebelled against God. As God's people, one aspect of their existence was not more spiritual than any other part. They worshiped God in everything they did, including taking care of Eden and loving each other.

But when Adam and Eve sinned in the Garden, their rebellion brought God's judgment upon themselves and the whole creation. First, God pronounced his judgment upon the serpent, the personification of Satan. But then he made an awesome promise in Genesis 3:15. "I will put enmity between you and the woman, and between your offspring and hers; he will crush your head, and you will strike his heel." This is the first promise of the gospel of God's grace to be found anywhere in the Scriptures. In essence, God promised a history-long struggle between two communities: the redeemed who love

God and the unredeemed who love self. This promise found its ultimate fulfillment when Jesus died upon the cross, thus destroying the works of the Devil and securing forgiveness and heaven for all of God's people.

God cursed life as Adam and Eve had come to know it. Childbearing and work, still filled with dignity, would now be marked with pain and hardship. The rest of the Bible records the spread of sin and death, like a cancerous disease, to every area of life. Relationships, work, the environment—nothing in God's creation was unaffected by the Fall. But the Scriptures also beautifully present the unfolding of God's incredible promise to destroy Satan and to redeem his people and his creation.

We jumped from Genesis to the last chapter of the last book of the Bible. In Revelation 22, we are given one of the clearest descriptions of heaven in the Scriptures: "No longer will there be any curse" (v. 3). This is huge! In other words, heaven will be the reversal of the Fall, the absence of every manifestation of sin and death. The curse will be lifted. No more pain, agony of labor, sweat, thorns, disease, sorrow, sin—only the fullness of God's grace and love will remain!

Joni Eareckson Tada wrote of this coming day with anticipation:

> I still can hardly believe it. I, with shriveled, bent fingers, atrophied muscles, gnarled knees, and no feeling from the shoulders down, will one day have a new body, light, bright, and clothed in righteousness—powerful and dazzling. . . . It's easy for me to be "joyful in hope," as it says in Romans 12:12, and that's exactly what I've been doing for the past twenty-odd years. My assurance of heaven is so alive that I've been making dates with friends to do all sorts of fun things once we get our new bodies. . . . I don't take these appointments lightly. I'm convinced these things will really happen.[2]

Everything that made human life miserable will be gone, and the fulfillment of God's magnificent design will be recaptured! A most glorious continuity will be realized between this world and the world to come. As God created things to be, so shall they be re-created! We will never be more fully human than in heaven. Princeton theologian A. A. Hodge encourages us:

> Heaven, as the eternal home of the divine Man (Jesus) and of all the redeemed members of the human race, must necessarily be thoroughly human in its structure, conditions, and activities. Its joy and its occupations must all be rational, moral, emotional, voluntary, and active. There must be the exercise of all faculties, the gratification of all tastes, the development of all talent capacities, the realization of all ideals. The reason, the intellectual curiosity, the imagination, the aesthetic instincts, the holy affections, the social affinities, the inexhaustible resources of strength and power native to the human soul, must all find in heaven exercise and satisfaction.[3]

Sounds a lot better than harps and halos, wouldn't you agree!

An Earthly Heaven

Next we looked at Revelation 21, in which John uses the language of "a new heaven and a new earth" to describe heaven (v. 1), an image that is rooted in the Old Testament Scriptures (Isa. 65:17–25). It made me think of the lush jungles and spectacular wildlife of South Africa that I saw a couple years ago, still unspoiled. What will it be like to see all of these animals living peacefully with one another again, even eating straw? But it's even more mind-boggling to contemplate Christians from our divided nation reconciled to one another, living as a community of equality, peace, and justice. What a vision!

The Heavenly City

One verse later John describes heaven as "the Holy City, the new Jerusalem" (Rev. 21:2). A good city is a creative place of peaceful community and dynamic interpersonal life. But this city will be unlike any other. It finds its glory in having God as its center. "Now the dwelling of God is with men, and he will live with them. They will be his people, and God himself will be with them and be their God" (Rev. 21:3).

The ancient city of Jerusalem in Israel will give way to the greater Jerusalem that "is coming down out of heaven." I tried to picture a whole city floating down from the sky. I wonder if Steven Spielberg would ever consider making a movie of that? The more Scotty and I talked, I began to realize that the Bible does not teach that heaven is an ethereal place somewhere out there beyond the Milky Way. Rather, it's a reality that God will bring about at the end of history. With this city will come the full vindication of Jesus, whose radiance will illuminate all things (Rev. 21:22). Richard Mouw described the glory of this coming day:

> The often subtle and always partial work that Jesus performed during his earthly ministry will someday be publicly completed in the midst of the transformed city. His Lordship over the whole cosmos must someday be made visible, must be openly vindicated. The authority of the Lamb must be made obvious to the entire creation.
>
> The Lamb is the lamp of the City who will draw all of the works of culture, and all rulers and peoples, to himself. He will do so, first of all as the true source to whom all things and peoples will return. "All things were made through him, and without him was not anything made that was made" (John 1:3) "for in him all things were created, in heaven and on earth, visible and invisible, whether thrones or dominions or principalities or authorities—all things were created through him and for him" (Col. 1:16). Jesus is the one who has been, from the very beginning, "upholding the universe by his word of power" (Heb. 1:3).[4]

A Garden City

Scotty and I started to link Scripture with Scripture as we pondered some of the connections between different biblical references to our eternal home. It seems appropriate to think of heaven as life in the Garden of Eden taken to the "nth" degree! A river brought life into the first Eden (Gen. 2:10–14), so in the "last Eden," described as a city, there will be "the river of the water of life, as clear as crystal, flowing from the throne of God and of the Lamb down the middle of the great street of the city" (Rev. 22:1–2). And access to the "tree of life," forbidden to Adam and Eve after the Fall (Gen. 3:22–24), will be given to all along with the open invitation to freely partake and enjoy its ever-changing yield of fruit (Rev. 22:2).

The first Eden, like the first Jerusalem, existed only as a shadow of what is to come. While the population of the first Eden consisted of only one couple, the landscape of heaven will be filled with numberless people, taken from every people group that has ever existed, all there because of the death and resurrection of Jesus. The "healing of the nations" (Rev. 22:2) occurs as a wondrous application of God's amazing gospel promise.

Bridal Affection

The final metaphor in John's awe-inspiring depiction of heaven is the most beautiful and astonishing. The people of God are presented as the bride of the Lamb (Rev. 19:5–9). John describes a great multitude who, "like the roar of rushing waters and like loud peals of thunder," shout with joy about the arrival of this day! A wedding feast inaugurates the beginning of the greatest marriage that could ever be hoped for or imagined. Whatever else heaven will be, it will most wondrously be an eternal celebration of the love shared between Jesus and his bride, the church. After John heard and saw this incredible vision of the wedding of the Lamb, he fell at the feet of the angel "to worship him." Some things should leave us in breathless, worshipful awe. This is certainly one of them.

Because of God's mercy, grace, and power—everything, once again, will be in perfect relationship, reintegrated according to his original design. And "there will be no more death or mourning or crying or pain, for the old order of things has passed away. He who was seated on the throne said, 'I am making everything new!'" (Rev. 21:4–5).

"Do you realize what all of this means, partner?" Scotty asked as we were just about exhausted from trying to take all of this in. "We usually only think of going to heaven when we die. But it's actually more scriptural to say that heaven is going to come to us! At the end of history Jesus is going to return and usher in this new heaven and new earth."

That sounded awesome, but it confused me too, so I asked, "Well, what about all of the people who have already died as believers? Where are they and what are they doing?"

"The Scriptures teach that they are very much with the Lord right now," Scotty assured me. "Paul says that 'to be away from the body' is to be 'at home with the Lord' (2 Cor. 5:8). They are in God's awesome presence, fully awake to his glory. But they are awaiting the return of Jesus to this world when the fullness of his kingdom will come and all Christians, from every period in history, will enjoy our complete inheritance together. As wonderful as it is to be currently with the Lord, no Christian has yet experienced the full wonders of the final estate."

Scotty:

How Then Shall We Live?

So how should a proper understanding of heaven affect the way we live our lives? What does heaven in the real world look like? There are many good answers to these questions, but three stand out:

1. A Living Hope

To understand what the Bible says about heaven is to find great encouragement and hope. History is going somewhere glorious! The best is yet to come! It's like being in the car en route to a much longed-for family vacation at the most wonderful place you could ever imagine. Only heaven will be far beyond what we could have ever hoped for, and our heavenly Father never tires of hearing us ask, "Are we there yet?" He understands our longings.

The apostle Paul is a great example of this living hope. He knew his true citizenship was in heaven, and he lived in eager expectation of the day when Jesus will return to transform everything, including our "lowly bodies" to be like his "glorious body" (Phil. 3:20–21).

Paul referred to our life in this world as an "earthly tent" and the life to come as "a building from God, an eternal house in heaven, not built by human hands" (2 Cor. 5:1). As a tentmaker, he knew that a tent is both mobile and temporary, appropriate for a sojourning existence. But a building is an established and permanent dwelling place, especially one from God!

As a boy, I used to love to camp out in my backyard. A friend and I would pitch my Cub Scout tent, complete with flooring and mosquito netting, just behind my house. It felt so good to look out from a tent flap, in the dead of night, amid all of the strange sounds, and see my *real* home. We need to keep our eyes fixed on the end of the journey so we can live with great passion and purpose now.

Our life in this world is filled with intense hope as we "groan, longing to be clothed with our heavenly dwelling" (2 Cor. 5:2). We are made for something far more grand than can possibly be realized in this world. That's why we can patiently endure all of the difficult parts of the journey.

There should be no doubt about this wonderful future, for, as Paul says, "Now it is God who has made us for this very purpose and has given us the Spirit as a deposit, guaranteeing what is to come" (2 Cor. 5:5). Hope is not a vague sense of possibility but a profound assurance of reality.

The gift of the Holy Spirit is our surety that we will enter into the fullness of heaven. When we bought our homes we had to put down earnest money. This deposit was our promise that we intended to render full payment on the closing date. In a similar way, God has placed his Spirit within our hearts, promising to bring to completion what he has begun. We can live with full assurance and peace about our eternal home closing! Nothing and no one can keep us from our final inheritance.

Paul got so excited about pondering our future as God's people that he found a tension in his heart. He said that it would be "better by far" to depart this life and to be with Christ. As a servant of Jesus, however, he realized that sharing the Good News of God's grace with others and building them up in the faith "is more necessary" for them (Phil. 1:23–24). The hope of heaven is meant to move us toward other-centered living.

2. The Stewardship of Time and Stuff

To think about heaven is also to be confronted with our mortality. It is startling for me to realize that I have already outlived my mother by ten years! She died when she was thirty-eight. King David's prayer speaks well for all of us, "You have made my days a mere hand-breadth; the span of my years is as nothing before you. Each man's life is but a breath" (Ps. 39:5).

Even if each of us gets our "three score and ten" (seventy) years, or eighty—or even a hundred—life is short. That is why Paul could speak of our "light and momentary troubles." In view of eternity, all trials are but brief interludes in the larger drama of "eternal glory," which "far outweighs them all" (2 Cor. 4:17). Thus Paul could say with confidence, "I consider that our present sufferings are not worth comparing with the glory that will be revealed in us" (Rom. 8:18).

The economy of heaven dramatically changes the value we place on things. Our treasures are seen in a different light. Jesus teaches us, "Do not store up for yourselves treasures on earth, where moth and rust destroy, and where thieves break in and steal. But store up for yourselves treasures in heaven, where moth and rust do not destroy, and where thieves do not break in and steal. For *where* your treasure is, there your heart will be also" (Matt. 6:19–21).

Notice that Jesus emphasizes the "where" of our treasure over the "what" of our treasure. Is our treasure on the earth or in heaven? Which realm has captured our imagination and passion, the kingdom of heaven or the kingdom of this world? Which ruler? When Paul thought about heaven, he thought about Jesus. Heaven is "heavenly" because Jesus is there in his fullness.

A passionate longing for heaven coupled with a linear view of history should propel us toward simple, unselfish living. Why is this not the case for so many Christians? C. S. Lewis, reflecting on our heavenly malaise, laments,

> If we consider . . . the staggering nature of the rewards promised in the Gospels, it would seem that our Lord finds our desires, not too strong, but too weak. We are half-hearted creatures, fooling about with drink and sex and ambition when infinite joy is offered us, like an ignorant child who wants to go on making mud pies in a slum because he cannot imagine what is meant by the offer of a holiday at the sea. We are far too easily pleased.[5]

To want heaven, however, is not to despise this world. Rather, it is to build a worldview and lifestyle that focuses on what matters to God. All of life can be divided into the perishable and the imperishable. Life is too short to be squandered.

3. Pushing Back the Effects of the Fall

Taken at face value, the biblical metaphors for heaven have huge implications concerning our call to be in the real world. Think about it. Since our final home is creation regained and restored, shouldn't we invest in renewing our world even now? Since God is in the process of making "all things new," let's join him!

As Christians, we are created, redeemed, and called to be God's representatives in all areas of life, bringing the salt and light of the gospel *everywhere*. As we have already noted, God created a world and called it good. He is re-creating the same world, and it will be even better.

There is profound truth in the great hymn title "This Is Our Father's World." Nothing our Father created is to be despised or taken lightly, for his creation is a manifestation of his glory. As King David sang, "The heavens declare the glory of God; the skies proclaim the work of his hands. Day after day they pour forth speech; night after night they display knowledge. There is no speech or language where their voice is not heard" (Ps. 19:1–3). Even the fallen world sounds an unmistakable clarion of praise to the wonders of our God.

Adam and Eve lived a spiritual life before God by being involved in all of his creation. Tending the Garden of Eden, naming the animals, exercising dominion over all things, loving each other—these were acts of worship as much as walking with God in the cool of the day.

But when the need for redemption came about through the Fall, our calling to be image bearers of God, vice-regents in God's creation, was not revoked. God restores our relationship to him through his grace, and then he liberates us to live for his glory. Society, the environment, culture, family, animal life, nature, government, leadership, creativity, music, art, science, education—God reigns over all these things, and he sends his children into the world to tend to them.

Unfortunately, many Christians make a distinction between the spiritual and the secular. For them, spiritual activity includes discipleship, the spiritual disciplines, religious activism, evangelism, missions, and church work. Everything else is categorized as being secular, or pertaining to the world. This leads to the wrong notion that our "ministry" and our "job" are two different things, unless we are "called to full-time Christian service."

But every Christian is "called." Our primary calling is to "love the Lord our God with all of our heart, all of our soul, all of our mind and all of our strength." We are to be consumed with the glory and grace of Jesus Christ. Secondly, Christians are to serve God in every area of life, culture, and vocation. Our Father sovereignly designs us, gives us talents, and places us in different areas of his creation.

Os Guinness masterfully describes this life of calling like this:

> Our primary calling as followers of Christ is by him, to him, and for him. First and foremost we are called to Someone (God), not to something (such as motherhood, politics, or teaching) or to somewhere (such as in the inner city or Outer Mongolia). Our secondary calling, considering who God is as sovereign, is that everyone, everywhere, and in everything should think, speak, live and act entirely for him. Secondary callings matter, but only because the primary calling matters.[6]

Our calling, therefore, is to know God as creator, redeemer, and re-creator.

This understanding should motivate us to reclaim the biblical doctrine of vocation. Martin Luther championed this cause for Christians in the sixteenth century. Luther, along with other leaders of the Reformation, longed for believers to rediscover elements of a biblical worldview that were lost during the Middle Ages. The Reformers believed that Christians should live in such a way as to "push back the effects of the Fall" in all spheres of life. God's glory is to be manifest in every square inch of the universe by each of his children—no exceptions.

A cobbler, who had joyfully embraced the gospel, approached the German reformer, "Master Luther, what am I to do with my life now?"

The liberated Luther responded, "Make good shoes and sell them at a fair price."

Luther stressed the dignity and importance of Christians doing all things from a heart of faith and with a commitment to excellence as a testimony to God's character. His simple response echoes the sentiments of Paul: "Whatever you do, work at it with all your heart, as working for the Lord, not for men, since you know that you will receive an inheritance from the Lord as a reward. It is the Lord Christ you are serving" (Col. 3:23–24).

In response to those who argue that the monastic and priestly callings please God more than others, Luther responded,

> The works of monks and priests, however holy and arduous they be, do not differ one whit in the sight of God from the works of the rustic laborer in the field or the woman going about her household tasks, but that all works are measured before God by faith alone.... Indeed, the menial housework of a manservant or maidservant is often more acceptable to God than all the fastings and other works of a monk or priest, because the monk or priest lacks faith.[7]

Our Christian subculture takes the cobbler's assumption a step further—or perhaps a step backward. The converted cobblers of our day (and their equivalent) assume that they should start making "Christian" shoes, or perhaps shoes just for Christians. But what is a Christian shoe? One that has a little "fish sign" pressed into the leather as a "witness tool," or a Bible verse embossed on the inside, proclaiming "with your feet fitted with the readiness that comes from the gospel of peace" (Eph. 6:15). The emergence of "Christian Yellow Pages" is a sad testimony to how we tend to withdraw from our culture into Christian cocoons rather than living "good lives among the pagans" (1 Peter 2:12).

Pastor and author Michael Scott Horton laments some of his early confusing days in the faith when

> Christians were expected to justify everything in their lives by its spiritual or evangelistic usefulness. At best, "secular" education, activities, vocations or pursuits were a necessary evil—in order to make a living, to be able to tithe and give to missionaries. If we discovered a little Rembrandt in a young artist at church, we put him in charge of the bulletin and (if he was really good) allowed him to paint the baptistry.[8]

What, then, does it look like to bring "heaven into the real world"? Two hundred years ago, William Wilberforce, a member of the English House of Parliament, was known to evangelical Christians as the politician who, against almost insurmountable odds, won the hotly contested battle for the abolition of slave trade in England. This brave man invested nearly fifty years of his life before he accomplished his goal. Few of us realize, however, that Wilberforce almost left politics before making his grand contribution to the moral and cultural reform of the British Empire.

When, at the age of twenty-five in 1785, Wilberforce committed his life to Christ, his first instinct was to leave politics for the "ministry." Like many of us, he assumed that the most important and holiest calling would be "professional ministry." Why spend his life in a secular job like politics when he could be preaching the gospel full-time? But none other than Pastor John Newton, a converted slave trader himself and author of the great hymn "Amazing Grace," convinced the young Wilberforce to perform his ministry in the realm of politics. History owes a great debt of gratitude to each of these men. May God be pleased to raise up another generation of Newtons and Wilberforces, compelled by the love of God and liberated by his grace to work hard for the transformation of life.

The day is coming when all sin, decay, and evil will be eradicated. A new heaven and a new earth will be ushered in, the eternal home of righteousness, peace, and joy. That day will not occur before the dramatic and glorious return of Jesus Christ. Until then, we are to move into the culture as representatives of our Creator-Redeemer Father—in the arts, science, business, politics, environmental studies, agronomy, law, philosophy, literature—in all areas. As we preach the gospel to the nations, we are to expand the presence of God's kingdom everywhere. The warfare will intensify as we get closer to the return of King Jesus, but we must not despair, give up in weariness, or retreat into a Christian cocoon. Remember, the King loves us! The kingdom has come and the kingdom is coming! We are not home yet, but we will be some day!

Both Steven and I wrestle with the question of heaven. How shall we invest the rest of our lives? How are we to be involved in the culture? In taking the gospel seriously, do we not open a Pandora's box? Even those questions do not convey the wildness of the questions we must ask as people who know the truth of heaven. To anticipate heaven is to have our very foundations shaken. It's to open the cage of the Lion of the Tribe of Judah, the King of the jungle, "the Lord of the whole Wood."

It was one of those days that fly fishermen dream about after watching all the Saturday morning fishing shows. Three of us, Scott Roley, Forest Reynolds, and I, headed out for the Caney Fork River, about an hour's drive from Nashville. We had been on this water many times before, but this day would be different.

Pulling up our waders and tying on the first fly of the day, we waded knee-deep into a couple of familiar spots not too far below the dam. The cool morning was heavy with dew, but a brilliant sun quickly moved us out of the warmth of our jackets and into our fishing vests, with all the little doodads, clips, and gear hanging off them. The first casts of the day yielded a few fish and an experienced fisherman's hunch from Forest: "Guys, this isn't bad, but let's go a little farther downriver and try a spot I saw last time I was here but haven't had a chance to fish."

Scott and I followed Forest several hundred yards to a place where the Caney narrows and, as we were about to find out, deepens considerably. Everything about this spot said "trout heaven." A deep, deep blue sky provided the backdrop for the tapestry of trellising tree limbs hanging over the glistening and inviting water. From ankles to knees to chest we waded out even as the current ran swifter and swifter.

Being the least experienced fly fisherman of the three, I got nervous. "Forest, where are you taking me? I'm having a hard time standing up. Are you and Scott setting me up?"

Both of them just laughed. "Let's have at it guys," Forest challenged us. "I smell fish."

We separated a safe casting distance from each other, and Scott and Forest began throwing our well-tied flies at every spot we hoped hungry trout might be waiting for lunch. I nervously positioned myself, sensing at any moment my waders would either fill up with water because we were in so deep, or else the rushing water would dislodge my footing and I would start floating yet further downstream! I am a natural born coward.

"Fish on!" Scott shouted. I watched as the trout exploded from the swirl, consuming Scott's well-presented fly. His line tightened and his rod bent double as his smile stretched wider than the Caney. With that first glorious cry came the rush of fisherman's adrenaline unique to this sport—I should say, this form of art. Quickly, I moved from fears to fishing. For the next two and a half hours we enjoyed the most incredible fly fishing I have ever experienced. Between the three of us, we caught nearly two hundred and fifty trout!

Everything we did worked, every fly we threw caught fish. It was almost comical. After a while we were tempted to cast under our arms or over our backs or with eyes closed. The fear I had of getting into the deeper rushing waters was exceeded exponentially by the delight of the fishing and the fellowship I shared with two dear brothers.

Other fly fishermen began showing up, sensing our good fortune. A few waded into the shallows, trying to figure out what we were doing, while some spin fishermen (God have mercy on them) started throwing spin baits, corn, and salmon eggs into the water in an attempt to catch the fish we were bringing in right and left. There were even a few bystanders without any fishing gear at all, simply watching our fun, taking pictures, and, perhaps, wondering what it would be like to be us! To enjoy what we enjoyed, however, you would have had to get into the water—chest deep—not ankle deep, not knee deep—but beyond-your-comfort-zone deep. I have no desire to fish from the safe confines of the bank anymore.

As I told this story in the pulpit one Sunday morning, with my fly rod in hand, Steven got the inspiration to write the song "Dive" for the *Speechless* record.

God calls each of us to abandon ourselves to his love as we dive into the bottomless waters of his goodness and resources. Through the gospel, he meets all of our needs and liberates us to enter into his plan for all of history and the world. It is our shared hope that this book leaves you with an intensified longing to get off of the banks of self-protection, fear, selfishness, and unbelief, and into the rushing rivers of God's grace. Such a move is not always easy or safe, but it is always right and good.

One of my favorite movies (and that of any fly fisherman) is *A River Runs Through It.* A river full of trout serves as the connecting metaphor, defining and holding together a family torn by the complexities, pains, and joys of life lived before the face of God. The Bible begins with the image of a river flowing through the Garden of Eden, watering God's new creation and refreshing his first son and daughter, Adam and Eve (Gen. 2:10), and breaking into four different headstreams that fed the surrounding regions. In the last chapter of the Bible we read of the "river of the water of life, . . . flowing from the throne of God and of the Lamb down the middle of the great street of the city" (Rev. 22:1–2).

Throughout history this river has been running as the gospel has gone out into the whole world. And in eternity, in the fullness of the new heavens and the new earth, this river will ever remind us and invite us to worship the God of all grace. This is the river "whose streams make glad the city of God" (Ps. 46:4). Come on in!

—Scotty Smith

Dive

The long awaited rains have fallen hard upon the thirsty
    ground
And carved their way to where the wild and rushing river
    can be found
And like the rains I have been carried here to where the
    river flows
My heart is racing and my knees are weak as I walk to the
    edge
I know there is no turning back once my feet have left the
    ledge

And in the rush I hear a voice that's telling me it's time to
    take the leap of faith
So here I go

I'm diving in, I'm going deep, in over my head I want to be
Caught in the rush, lost in the flow, in over my head I want
    to go
The river's deep, the river's wide, the river's water is alive
So sink or swim, I'm diving in

There is a supernatural power in this mighty river's flow
It can bring the dead to life, It can fill an empty soul
(when it washes through a soul)
And gives a heart the only thing worth living and worth
    dying for
But we will never know the awesome power of the Grace of
    God
Until we let ourselves get swept away into this Holy flood
So if you'll take my hand we'll close our eyes and count to
    three
and take the leap of faith
Come on let's go

I'm diving in, I'm going deep, in over my head I want to be
Caught in the rush, lost in the flow, in over my head I want
    to go
The river's deep, the river's wide, the river's water is alive
So sink or swim, I'm diving in

acknowledgments

Thank you to Scotty Smith for faithfully leading the way through this exciting and frightening new writing frontier for me. This book and the thoughts in it would certainly not be a reality without your encouragement, your wisdom, and most importantly your friendship. I love you brother!

Thanks to all the treasured friends who have journeyed with Mary Beth and me through the process of writing this book and making the recording by the same title. Through your love and friendship I have come to a deeper understanding of just how amazing God's grace truly is.

To Dan Coley and Al Andrews for challenging me to allow myself to be speechless, Ray Mullican for praying, Geoff Moore for listening and always bringing a smile to my face, Tim Burke for helping me remember what it is to hope, Al Henson for mentoring me at such a vital time in my life.

Thank you to Ann Spangler for believing that this book should be written and to Bob Hudson for his patient and masterful editing of this "first time author."

Thanks to Dan Raines for bringing all the pieces together as you do so well and to Melissa Banek for trying so hard to keep me organized.

Thanks to my mom, dad, and brother Herbie for starting me out on the journey into the unsearchable riches of God's grace and mercy.

I must try to say thank you to my precious wife Mary Beth and our three children Emily, Caleb, and Will Franklin. Even though my words will always fall inadequately short, I want to say that it has been through you that God has shown me the clearest outlines of this amazing and astonishing grace. I love you more than my songs or my words could ever tell you.

Finally, thank you to the one reading these words right now. The fact that you are holding this book in your hand is a humbling honor and a tremendous privilege. Thank you for letting me share these thoughts and experiences. I pray that your time invested in reading this book will be rewarded with a fresh new sense of astonishment and that by God's grace, we will grasp how wide, how long, how deep, and how high the love of Christ is for us.

—Steven

With special thanks to Darlene, my loving wife of twenty-seven years—my son Scott, my daughter Kristin, and son-in-law Matt. I love each of you more than I can adequately convey and am so proud of each of you.

To Steven Curtis—thanks my dear brother for your long-term friendship and ongoing encouragement, both of which give me courage to "Dive" and to dance.

To the family of Christ Community Church for the gift of a sabbatical season that provided the occasion for the writing of this book and, more importantly, for the renewing of my heart by the God of all grace. Thanks for the freedom you give me to groan and grow in grace with you.

To Ann Spangler and Bob Hudson at Zondervan for your prodding, encouragement, and great skill. And thanks to Arlene Fulmer and Diane LeJeune for your labor of love in helping Steven and me with the manuscript in its earliest stages.

Special thanks to the following who helped me this past year to access the riches of God's grace afresh: Hollie Brown and Belinda Johnson, Parke and Rhonda Brown, Brevard and Jane Haynes, Harry and Mary Beth Shields, Gary and Gale Kennedy, John and Mary Love Patton, Bob and Amy Jones, Mike and Cindy Hottinger, Buddy Greene, Al Andrews, Clyde Godwin, David Hampton . . . the Covenant Seminary community, and, as always, Scott Roley.

—Scotty

Chapter One: Speechless

1. Stacey and Paula Rhinehart, *Living in Light of Eternity* (Colorado Springs: NavPress, 1986), 30.

Chapter Two: The Dance of the Lord

1. C. S. Lewis, *Letters to Malcolm: Chiefly on Prayer* (New York: Harcourt Brace Jovanovich, 1964), 45.
2. *Heidelberg Catechism,* 1563, Q. 60, 1975 translation.
3. John Owen, *Communion with God,* ed. R. J. K. Law (Edinburgh: Banner of Truth, 1991), 117.
4. Henri Nouwen, *The Return of the Prodigal Son* (New York: Image/Doubleday, 1994), 40, 42.
5. Søren Kierkegaard, quoted in Rebecca Manley Pippert, *Hope Has Its Reasons* (New York: Harper & Row, 1989), 17.

Chapter Three: Hope for Returning Prodigals and Recovering Pharisees

1. Rose Marie Miller, *From Fear to Freedom* (Wheaton, Ill.: Harold Shaw, 1994), 4.
2. Jerry Bridges, *The Discipline of Grace* (Colorado Springs: NavPress, 1994), 18.
3. Henri Nouwen, *The Return of the Prodigal* (New York: Doubleday, 1992), 76.

Chapter Four: New Creation

1. Rebecca Manley Pippert, *Hope Has Its Reasons* (New York: Harper & Row, 1989), 14.
2. Abraham Kuyper, quoted in Richard Mouw, *When the Kings Come Marching In* (Grand Rapids: Eerdmans, 1989), 67.

Chapter Six: Models and Mentors: Those Who Shape Us

1. Oswald Chambers, *My Utmost Devotional Bible* (Nashville, Thomas Nelson, 1982), 235.
2. Eugene Peterson, quoted in Ken Gire, *Windows of the Soul* (Grand Rapids: Zondervan, 1996), 76.

Chapter Seven: That's What Friends Are For

1. David Hansen, *The Art of Pastoring* (Downers Grove, Ill.: InterVarsity, 1994), 117–18.
2. Jerry and Mary White, *Friends and Friendship* (Colorado Springs: NavPress, 1982), 13.
3. Gordon MacDonald, *Renewing Your Spiritual Passion* (Nashville: Oliver-Nelson, 1989), 171.
4. Patrick Morley, *The Man in the Mirror* (Grand Rapids: Zondervan, 1998), 117.
5. Larry Crabb, *The Silence of Adam* (Grand Rapids: Zondervan, 1995), 161.

Chapter Eight: Freedom to Hurt and Grieve

1. Ken Gire, *Windows of the Soul* (Grand Rapids: Zondervan, 1996), 102.
2. C. S. Lewis, *A Grief Observed* (New York: Bantam, 1976), 53–54.
3. Nicholas Wolterstorff, *Lament for a Son* (Grand Rapids: Eerdmans, 1997).

Chapter Nine: Infectious Grace

1. John Stott, "The Bible in World Evangelization," *Perspectives on the World Christian Movement*, ed. R. D. Winter and S. C. Hawthorne (Pasadena: William Carey Library, 1981), 4.

Chapter Ten: Living in Light of Heaven

1. John Stott, *Authentic Christianity*, ed. Timothy Dudley-Smith (Downers Grove, Ill.: InterVarsity, 1995), 403.
2. Joni Eareckson Tada, *Heaven: Your Real Home* (Grand Rapids: Zondervan, 1995), 53–55.
3. A. A. Hodge, *Evangelical Theology* (Carlisle, Pa.: Banner of Truth, 1976), 403.
4. Richard Mouw, *When the Kings Come Marching In* (Grand Rapids: Eerdmans, 1989), 66.

5. C. S. Lewis, *The Weight of Glory* (Grand Rapids: Eerdmans, 1949), 13.

6. Os Guinness, *The Call* (Nashville: Word, 1998), 31.

7. Martin Luther, quoted in Os Guinness, *The Call* (Nashville: Word, 1998), 34.

8. Michael Scott Horton, *Where in the World Is the Church?* (Chicago: Moody, 1995), 9–10.

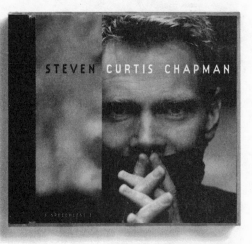

We want to hear from you. Please send your comments about this
book to us in care of the address below. Thank you.

ZondervanPublishingHouse
Grand Rapids, Michigan 49530
http://www.zondervan.com